D0709280

Swimming with Elephants

Center Point
Large Print

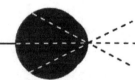

**This Large Print Book carries the
Seal of Approval of N.A.V.H.**

Swimming with Elephants

MY UNEXPECTED PILGRIMAGE
FROM PHYSICIAN TO HEALER

SARAH BAMFORD SEIDELMANN

CENTER POINT LARGE PRINT
THORNDIKE, MAINE

The text of this Large Print edition is unabridged.
In other aspects, this book may vary
from the original edition.
Printed in the United States of America
on permanent paper.
Set in 16-point Times New Roman type.

ISBN: 978-1-68324-641-1

Library of Congress Cataloging-in-Publication Data

Names: Seidelmann, Sarah Bamford, author.
Title: Swimming with elephants : my unexpected pilgrimage from
    physician to healer / Sarah Bamford Seidelmann.
Description: Large print edition. | Thorndike, Maine :
    Center Point Large Print, 2018.
Identifiers: LCCN 2017046540 | ISBN 9781683246411
    (hardcover : alk. paper)
Subjects: LCSH: Seidelmann, Sarah Bamford. | Women shamans—
    Biography. | Women physicians—Biography. | Large type books.
Classification: LCC BF1611 .S45 2018 | DDC 201/.44092 [B]—dc23
LC record available at https://lccn.loc.gov/2017046540

For Mollie Catherine Ashworth

Contents

PART THREE: INDIA

PART FOUR: RETURN HOME

Author's Note

This memoir accurately reflects my own experience. I have reconstructed the story from my memories, my journal entries, and from my conversations with the characters involved. All names and details are real except for several of the participants in my travels to India and in my residency training. As the friends in my brain trust are fond of saying: you cannot make this stuff up. I have occasionally compressed and shifted the chronology of some events for clarity.

If you are in search of an excellent curriculum and ethical teachers to learn more about shamanism, I heartily encourage you to check out the Foundation for Shamanic Studies at *shamanism.org*. Originated, researched, and developed over nearly fifty years by anthropologist Michael Harner—the pioneer of contemporary shamanism—the Foundation's training can offer students like you the opportunity to learn and practice authentic, powerful, and effective shamanic healing methods. Their decades-long and broad-based effort continues to provide an immense contribution toward healing humankind and the Beasties and the Earth we all share.

Introduction

Safety is all well and good;
I prefer freedom.

E. B. White, *The Trumpet of the Swan*

I was gently eased into chaos by a sneaking sensation that I was no longer doing the work I was meant to do. My career in medicine, that had formerly thrilled me, began to feel like a prison. As it turned out, the door to my metaphorical jail cell had always been ajar, waiting for me to leave it and explore. Instead of wandering out, I could have chosen to reupholster my office chair in an adorable European chintz with a pattern of dancing pugs—pugs, after all, are incredibly whimsical. Through my lifelong enthusiasm for interior design, I knew that changing a room could change your life. At some point, however, I realized that it would be dangerous for me to stay. Material shifts are useful; but only changes at the level of spirit endure.

What my soul truly craved was freedom.

I was dying—at least, the externally driven, board-certified part of me was dying. I felt called to do something else. Precisely what that something else was, however, eluded me. I knew something was wrong, and I was filled with self-doubt.

Eventually, I left medicine to pursue a radically different path. What did I do to arrive at that path? A better question might be, what didn't I do?

I danced with sacred stones, meditated with mantras, faced my shadow, spent dozens of hours traveling to sacred realms via drumbeat to meet helpful spirits, tramped on trails while communicating with the wild, embraced a rescued mustang, lay on a tarp in the desert while being examined by twelve strangers, sold half of our possessions in a public sale, and had bones thrown for me by African shamans.

All of these strange activities played an important part in the messy process of finding my connection to the Divine and learning to trust its guidance. Most people, my friend Suzi teases me, would never have taken these extreme measures. Others may not long to cavort with a gazillion Hindu pilgrims on the banks of the Ganges river, but my hope is that my story inspires you, dear reader, to find your own path to freedom.

With hindsight, I recognize that my distress with others' suffering was my call to the Hero's journey. Faced with the enormity of my discomfort, I refused at first. It took me years to understand how to change my answer from "no" to "yes."

If you decide to say "yes" to your own soul's calling, I've got one question for you:

How good are you willing to let it get?

PART ONE

Angry Bears

All doors are hard to unlock
until you have the key.

Robert C. O'Brien,
Mrs. Frisby and the Rats of NIMH

CHAPTER 1

Spirit of the Bear

"You would not have called to me unless
I had been calling to you," said the Lion.

C. S. Lewis, *The Silver Chair*

The persistent thrum of the drum urges me
forward. In my mind's eye, I go to a canyon
in Utah that is walled by soaring cliffs. The
ground is dry and covered in low grasses and
herbaceous plants. The soft morning air smells of
pungent sage. I decide to travel down a gravel-
floored tunnel from a cave I conjure up from
memory. My bare feet connect with the cool stone
tunnel floor. The walls are damp and covered
with droplets of water as I feel along them with
my hands on the way down, down, down.

As I step out of the tunnel onto soft sand
and enter the Lower World, I see a red-winged
blackbird—the kind that has surrounded me in
the marsh lately. Per-co-cheee! When I ask her
silently if she is the animal who can help me,
she indicates "no" with a slight head movement
but invites me to follow her. She brings me to

a bear. I *feel* her—her large claws and leathery pads. She allows me to place my hands over her broad, upturned paws, and I can sense her immense feminine strength. Then she wraps her arms around me.

In her embrace, I ask this bear: "Why are you here? How are you here to help me?" She takes me into her cave and soothes me, rubs my back, and tells me: "All will be well on this new journey." I feel loved by the divine kind of mother you can only conjure up in dreams, one who loves you for exactly who you are, *no matter what.* She turns and shows me an image of a huge rhinoceros (on a flip chart, strangely enough) and says: "You're in the process of becoming more like the rhino—thick-skinned and peaceful."

Strangely, I believe in this mother bear. I feel as if my experience with her, on some level, is more legitimate than any experience I've ever had in "real life." As the drumming comes to a close, I return from my first visit to the Lower World feeling calmer and more peaceful. And I find that I also believe a bit more in myself.

I recall a time, decades ago, when I was in college, and my dad and I camped in the Boundary Waters of Minnesota. In the fall, the two of us backpacked on the Border Route trail. At night, we scarfed up the freeze-dried food we'd packed, famished after hauling our gear eight or nine miles along the hilly trails. After dinner, we strung our packs up high in the trees for safekeeping and built a fire for warmth against those cold autumn nights.

That year, there had been some alarming and unusual bear attacks in the area and I remember wishing that we had brought a can of mace or something. How was I going to defend myself or my dad if a deranged bear attacked? One night, we saw what we called the "spirit of the bear"—a little glowing face in the embers of the campfire. It was subtle and flickered in and out. A nose, dark ears, and two glowering eyes.

Dad chuckled and reminded me about the Virgin of Suyapa, the patroness of Honduras, a deity revered for her healing abilities, who had first revealed herself to only a few individuals. "Maybe when they first recognized the Suyapa, it was a bit like our little bear here in the campfire," he said, smiling. The moment suddenly felt sacred, as if we had seen a vision.

Until that moment, I had forgotten about Suyapa, a deity to whom, at thirteen, I had felt shyly drawn. While I was working on a medical mission with my dad in Honduras, I bought a tiny gold pendant in her image for myself with money I had saved up from babysitting. Despite years of attending an Episcopal church, Suyapa felt holy to me in a way that Jesus had yet to do.

The campfire spirit wasn't the only bear that

had appeared in my life, however. I suddenly remembered that I'd been known as "Sarah Bear" throughout high school, because, for a year, I had played the bear mascot for our sports teams. And while out jogging in my neighborhood just last year, I had come across a mother bear and two cubs. Were these merely coincidences? Was I simply making up this connection? Somehow it felt like more than that. A bear? Yes. In fact, she had been with me all along.

My first visit to the Lower World brought my connection to Mother Bear back into my life. This place, recognized by many shamanic cultures as an earthly realm filled with loving and compassionate spirits, is typically accessed through a tunnel in the ground. In fact, there are three "worlds" recognized by shamans all over the earth. The Upper and Lower Worlds are places where you can seek loving and compassionate spirits. The spirits in the Upper World tend to be in human form, while those in the Lower World tend to be in animal form. The Middle World, which includes the earth, the sky, the sun, the moon, and the stars—essentially the Universe— holds a mixed bag of spirits, some of whom are suffering, not loving and compassionate. This is not a place you normally go to discover a spirit guide.

The wise men and women known as shamans

who purposely journey to communicate with the spirits truly fascinated me. These unique individuals can act as conduits for the spirits, allowing healing and the transmission of information to help themselves and their communities. They can speak with the leaping leopard, the mouse, the trees; they collaborate with each spirit. I found that I was hungry for the kind of knowledge these shamans seemed to possess and eager to bring their wisdom into my life. I was ready to set out on this path—ready to enter the unknown. How had my life brought me to this realization? Like all important journeys, it can only be understood backwards.

CHAPTER 2

Hitched and Launched

Even between the closest people infinite
distances exist, a marvelous living side-
by-side can grow up for them, if they
succeed in loving the expanse between
them, which gives them the possibility of
always seeing each other as a whole and
before an immense sky.

Rainer Maria Rilke,
Letters to a Young Poet

My first day at medical school, I pointed
out Mark to my parents in our class photo
book. He was six feet four inches tall—a good
eight inches taller than I was—reserved and
self-possessed, with large and kind blue eyes. I
tried to make eye contact with him in the student
lounge and in the hallway, but he was tough to
reach. This wasn't going to be easy. I joined
intramural soccer to stalk him, even though I'd
never played the game in my life. At our first
practice, I casually asked around—"Where's
Seidelmann?"—and was told that he'd hurt his

ankle playing volleyball and was out for the season.

I quit soccer on the spot, found Mark in the gym nearby, introduced myself, and helped him hobble to his car. He never really had a chance.

Weeks later, we had an awkward, yet strangely satisfactory, exchange at a Halloween party—I was Peter Pan in green tights; Mark was a Kabuki warrior in a silk robe and white face paint. Invisible sparks flew as we slowly tossed a Nerf ball back and forth while speaking of innocuous things like our shared love of the British New Wave band Modern English. A few days later, he called and asked me out.

He took me to a bar that was filled with tattooed bikers sporting bandanas and chains. We—a khaki- and Shetland sweater–sporting duo—definitely did not belong. The bikers soon returned to pounding their pitchers of beer, perhaps satisfied that we weren't missionaries. Mark's choice of venue startled me, because I'd heard from a friend that Mark's father was a Lutheran pastor. But I enjoyed being surprised like that. When I asked why he'd chosen a biker bar, he shrugged and offered: "The beer is cheap."

Five dates later—I almost gave up—we hadn't even kissed. On our sixth date, over a stir-fry Mark had expertly fixed in his apartment, we spoke of many serious things. Then he abruptly lunged at me. We began kissing and didn't stop, quickly falling from our chairs to the floor and rolling around until we eventually knocked the record player off the shelf. Later, he told me: "I had to do *something!* You wouldn't stop talking about Gorbachev and Gandhi."

There were a few hiccups during our courtship. Mark was really worried that, when he introduced me to his parents, my propensity for salty language would put them off. I wasn't known for my verbal restraint. All the way down to Minneapolis, he admonished me to avoid even the words "God" or "damn." I restrained myself as best I could and somehow made it through the weekend. His parents were lovely. Eighteen months later, we were married.

Newly married zeal prompted me to share with Mark my fantastic dream: *Now we can go to India!* After all, we were free—no kids or real jobs yet. I was only twenty-four. He was twenty-six. A chunk of time off between medical school and residency seemed a perfect opportunity to take the epic journey to India I'd always imagined. Think of it—the birthplace of Gandhi!

"We'll go together!" I exclaimed, after presenting my vision of India to my beloved in our freeway-hugging apartment, frugally adorned with unfinished pine Adirondack chairs. Mark looked at me, bewildered, and said: "What? I have no interest in going to India. Why would you want to go *there?*"

We'd just returned from our honeymoon, which preceded our clinical rotations as medical students in Minneapolis. I was simultaneously excited about the life we were building together and apprehensive about what lay ahead. I thought India would give me something to look forward to. India was the farthest place I could imagine from where I stood as a freshly minted wife and soon-to-be MD. I longed to explore places that were foreign in every way before settling down to a "normal" life. Maybe it was just a longing to be free again—unfettered, even if just for a little while—after the rigors of medical school.

I wasn't yet aware that India was calling to me from a more subtle place—beyond the predictable chicken josh, colorful saris, and winking mirrors. Watching the film *Gandhi* with a few close friends in high school had struck a deep chord in us. We had dubbed ourselves the "Gandhettes" as a sort of loose show of affiliation with this amazing man and his mission. A part of me wanted never to forget this great leader, his warm smile, and the equanimity that fairly beamed out of him despite all the violence and suffering he saw and endured.

Because of this, I was blindsided and baffled by Mark's response. Who *wouldn't* want to go to India? Surely this wasn't the adventurous guy

I'd married a few weeks before, the man with whom I was to live out my decades in harmony. Mark was still talking, but I had tuned him out, until he said: "It seems odd that you'd actually *enjoy* a place like India," implying that extreme poverty, crowds, and general disorder didn't seem compatible with who I was. I was crushed. Didn't he know by now that I loved mayhem of all sorts?

In the months that followed, I began to wonder if we had made a huge mistake. Maybe we had rushed into marriage too quickly. In fact, that first year of marriage proved a most difficult year for us.

"This red pepper looks awesome for dinner tonight," I said, tossing it into the cart.

"Did you see the price? I don't think so," Mark said, lifting it out and putting it back on the pile. "We can just do a green pepper—they're half the price."

I wasn't used to conferring over vegetable purchases. In retrospect, I realized that, during our courtship, I had often footed the bill for things Mark didn't deem necessary—new CDs, red peppers, and take-out pizza. After a year of marriage, however, we seemed to pass some significant milestone, and it got a bit easier.

CHAPTER 3

Realization and Refusal

For the hero who refuses the call to
adventure, all he can do is create new
problems for himself and await the
gradual approach of his disintegration.

Joseph Campbell, *The Hero with a
Thousand Faces*

A few months after our honeymoon, I found
myself on the hospital ward with Dean, a
second-year resident in internal medicine. I was
a third-year medical student, and this particular
hospital rotation was pushing me to my limits
intellectually, physically, and spiritually.

In order to finish rounds on my patients before
Dean arrived, I left our apartment at 4:30 in the
morning, arriving in the Intensive Care Unit
around 5:00. I did a physical exam on our first
patient and then sat at the desk poring over the
chart, which was three inches thick, trying to
decipher the cryptic notes left by specialists,
following up on labs and culture results, noting
all recorded vital signs, and making sure that

I hadn't missed anything before I wrote up my assessment and plan, which would be reviewed by my resident and the attending physician.

But these routine aspects of medicine weren't what was most difficult for me. What stopped me in my tracks was something for which I'd received no formal training.

One morning, I was faced with a patient—a recently divorced twenty-nine-year-old mother of three—who was on an experimental bone-marrow transplant protocol for Stage IV breast cancer. We'd flooded her body with incredibly toxic chemotherapy to obliterate her tumor, but the destruction was nonselective. For the treatment to succeed, her native bone-marrow elements had to regenerate in order for her to survive. But her platelets (the tiny cell fragments that help blood to clot) had dropped to almost nil and were refusing to recover.

Dean and I stood by her bed and stared at her frail frame covered in heavy blankets. We were fairly close as we spoke with her, maybe three feet away, but I felt as if we might just as well have been talking to her from behind a thick glass wall. "Your platelets remain low," Dean said. "But we're hoping to get a bigger bump with today's transfusion." I had no words, so I just smiled weakly. I felt so separate, as if I couldn't really touch the problems she was facing. Or was it that she was feeling the distance that separated us? Had she already given up?

Despite the thousands of memorized medical facts and concepts that swam through my brain, the skills of my admirable resident, and the collective wisdom of modern medicine, it seemed to me that we were *missing the point.* She could very well be dying. How could we help her with that?

This patient haunted me all the way home that night, and I began to question everything, including what I was doing and what modern medicine dictated we do. I found myself wondering what it would be like if it were my job to talk with this patient about death. What would I say to her?

I was reassured by the way Dean had spoken to her in a soft, measured voice. I loved him for that. He had a quiet stillness. His bustling-physician self seemed to recede, and he was able to line up with the patient perfectly, the way a lake merges with its shore. Though we didn't talk about it, I could feel that he sensed a need to treat her with all the tenderness he could muster. I wanted to ask him what he was feeling about her, but we were so busy that the time never came.

Days later, while Dean and I were sprinting toward a new consultation through an echo-filled stairwell that reeked of linoleum and fresh paint, we received a voice page from the ward. Our frail patient had bled to death early that morning. Though her recovery had been very uncertain, it still caught us off guard. We paused for a moment, sitting down on the rubbery stairs, and allowed our tears to come. For this, I was grateful. I later learned that this was rare. Most rotations I would do, and most residents, didn't allow you to stop for a moment of humanity like this.

Months later, at the University of Minnesota, a six-week hematology/oncology rotation left me emotionally shattered. During my exit interview, the attending physician, whom I'd barely met, asked me for feedback. As he waited for my response, his eyes looked searchingly at me and then down at the form he needed to fill out. I couldn't get the words to come out. I unexpectedly took in a sharp breath, and the dam inside me broke. I began to sob, seized by a sorrow so deep and painful that I was overcome by it.

Remembered scenes flashed through my mind: the liver-transplant patient who seemed more dead than alive, the families wiped out by grief, the way patients were callously treated by the angry and dismissive resident with whom I had been paired. Each room we walked into had felt so heavy. The suffering had felt unbearable to me. It had taken everything I had just to stand there and look these patients in the eye. Our visits seemed to provide no apparent relief.

After a few minutes of uncontrolled weeping and shuddering, the baffled attending physician handed me a box of tissues. Though I was trying desperately to control my emotions so I could tell him what I'd experienced, I just couldn't stop. I gestured helplessly toward the door, grabbed my bag, and escaped to keen in the privacy of a bathroom stall down the hall. I waited until it was quiet in the hallway, and, my tears subsided, I slipped out of the building.

Our internships took a new and deeper toll on Mark and placed an intense pressure to perform on me. One Saturday at home, we got into an argument, and I became furious with him. The only thing I could think of to exact revenge was to take his beloved houseplant and drop it unceremoniously into the sink with a crash. Plant violence was, apparently, the best I could come up with. He was understandably angry. But I was extremely surprised when he charged toward me. Instinctively, I began to run, but he tackled me as I tried to escape up the carpeted stairs. I was shocked and scared. Mark was one of the kindest and calmest people I knew. What was happening to us? Later, I told him that, if he ever grabbed me like that or tackled me again, I would have to leave.

After that, Mark became even more distant and unavailable, and seemed to undergo a complete change in personality. I knew that working a hundred hours a week could do that to a person, but I became truly worried. I talked Mark into seeing a couples' therapist on one of our rare days off. After thirty minutes of listening to us, the therapist said: "I see a lot of couples, and I can tell that you two love each other very much. You're going to be just fine." I drove away feeling slightly better, but wondered how she could be so sure.

After the death of my bone-marrow-transplant patient and my own disturbing discovery that I was ill-prepared to serve patients at the level I sensed they needed, I decided to sidestep the whole troublesome aspect of caring for patients personally and chose pathology as a specialty.

By choosing pathology, I committed to mastering something tangible and dodged the most painful and confusing aspect of medicine— addressing the patient's emotional and spiritual needs. As a pathologist, I only had to look at slivers and bits under a microscope and occasionally do a few autopsies.

But I discovered that I enjoyed pathology immensely. The doctors were brilliant and collaborative. It was also, at times, very exciting. During one typical intraoperative neurosurgery consultation, I heard:

"Mary, get the down here to the multiheaded

scope! We've got a doozy of a brain biopsy, and I need you *now!*"

Mary skidded into the room moments later, threw down her glasses, and slid into a chair. She put her eyes up to the scope and demanded clarification: "What the fuck are we looking at here?"

"Twenty-seven-year-old frontal lobe mass with necrosis," the other pathologist replied.

Mary immediately began directing the examination like a boot-camp drill sargeant: "Okay, okay, move to the right . . . no, left . . . okay, *there* . . . go down on that cell . . . I need to see it closer, Bob!" It fascinated me to watch these brilliant people wrestle with significant diagnostic problems and collaborate to provide the very best answer for the patient.

Another instructor from medical school was very influential in my decision to become a pathologist. Most medical school professors I had met were introverted types who enjoyed the symphony, a good Sudoku, and quiet nights at home. But this physically imposing guy with a huge bald head frequently said outrageous and shocking things. In fact, sometimes I wonder whether he was, in fact, the only reason I was initially drawn into pathology. I remember one after-class party at which he invited unsuspecting students to look at photographs he had taken under his microscope, challenging them to determine how the patient had contracted the infection. Baffled, the students peered with great intellectual interest at the clumped patterns of bacteria, each wanting to come up with the correct answer. It took a while for most to realize that he had used patterns of a bacteria known to be transmitted sexually to spell out "fucking."

Pathologists are "the doctors' doctors." They consult with all other physicians, providing diagnostic clarity where possible and diagnostic possibilities where it is not. As I watched pathologists interact with surgeons and oncologists, I saw how important their role was and thought that, perhaps if I worked hard, I could be helpful as well.

At its most essential, pathology is good pattern-recognition. During my student rotation, I got feedback that I was showing promise as a diagnostician, and it encouraged me. As a pathologist, I thought, I could avoid the discomfort of witnessing human suffering, be a mother who gets to see her children (at twenty-six, these children were still notional, but pathologists were purported to have fairly regular hours), and I could be myself and swear like a sailor whenever I needed to.

For that first year, I lived, breathed, ate, and slept the study of disease and how to make a solid diagnosis. It was like learning a whole new language in which I needed to become fluent—

fast. I loved staring for hours at each week's ten "unknown" cases, trying to make the most accurate diagnosis. It was a little like trying to remember the name of a specific wallpaper pattern (like Farrow and Ball's Toile Trellis). Each time, the details are similar, but not identical, to patterns you've seen before.

CHAPTER 4

Lightening the Load

Until one is committed, there is
hesitancy, the chance to draw back,
always ineffectiveness . . . the moment
one definitely commits oneself, then
Providence moves too.

W. H. Murray, *The Scottish Himalayan
Expedition*

After five years of residency and a few years
practicing in Wisconsin, we were thrilled to
find jobs in Duluth and return "home." We had
begun our family by adopting a son, George,
during our final years of residency. By the time
we had settled into our practice, George was
four and a half, and we were ready to adopt our
daughter, Katherine. I loved being a mom but
often felt lonely and stressed. Mark left around
7:00 in the morning and didn't come home until
between 9:00 and 11:00 most nights. On-call
weekends were worse. I felt like a single parent
who had her own intensely demanding job.

One night while we were lying in bed together

after a particularly draining week, I tried to open a conversation.

"Isn't there any way you could see fewer patients or lighten your load somehow?" I pleaded. "I can't go on like this." I reminded him of how, in residency, we had said that we wanted to work part time, share parenting, and have a *life.*

"It's not easy," Mark said defensively. "We have to see all the patients and consults. It all takes time."

When I begged, he promised that he'd lighten his schedule, and he did—for a few months. Then, slowly, his workload ratcheted up again. When I spoke to the other spouses in his practice, they seemed frustrated as well, but also resigned to the fourteen-hour days. I frequently ended the day in tears—exhausted, confused, and lonely.

My days often began in the dark. Mark had usually already left to complete his early hospital rounds before his clinic started. Katherine, by then a toddler, got a diaper change and some kisses before I parked her sleepy self on my hip. Then I rousted George, and we headed down to the kitchen. Both kids were already dressed—they slept in their street clothes, a trick I'd devised in residency to avoid the morning dressing fiasco.

After assessing the condition of Katherine's hair to determine whether I could avoid a hair-combing battle, I was usually confronted with demands from George to be picked up early, complaining that he was always one of the last kids to be retrieved from childcare. Thinking about my packed schedule, I promised to be there as early as I could, with a knot beginning to form in my stomach as I admitted to myself that I'd probably be one of the last parents there again. Then we went through the wrestling match required to get sunscreen applied—something we all hated with the white-hot passion of a thousand suns.

After a quick breakfast, we leaped into the van and sped off to "before-school care" for George. Then I drove across town to bring Katherine to her childcare, which was located in a church near the hospital. I often left saying a silent thanks for the loving care she received there and feeling ashamed that I was too busy to give her that care. At times, I wished I were a daycare provider and not stuck at the hospital, thinking what a delight it would be—however challenging—to hang out all day with my daughter. Then I got back in my car and headed to the hospital. Sometimes tears sprang up—tears I quickly swallowed. I had to keep moving. Some days, I even had to admit that it was a *relief* to drop off my kids, because I felt so unqualified to meet their needs in my harried state.

At night, I repeated this whole process in

reverse. Occasionally, Mark escaped work to join us for dinner or we met him at the hospital cafeteria. But, more often, he and I only saw each other briefly at night when he finally got home.

At one pain-filled point, after a particularly difficult week of solo parenting, I confronted Mark in desperation. "If I'm going to do this all on my own," I complained, "I might as well drop any expectation that you're going to be part of our lives."

"I don't really appreciate being threatened like that," Mark replied. "I know things need to change, and I'm working on it."

Frankly, I was grateful that Mark didn't get angry with me in the moment; I also felt guilty for pulling out the big guns. I was beginning to realize that looking to him to solve this problem was a mistake. I wanted a partner to help me carry the load, but I still wasn't sure how to proceed.

During that extremely lonely period, I envied people who seemed to believe in God, despite the challenging circumstances of their lives. They seemed calm and sure. But I had no such refuge, because, frankly, I couldn't fathom that kind of belief. I cynically suspected that religion was just a misguided way to help people cope with the vast unknowns in life. I tried to discuss this openly with my closest friend, Suzi, a grounded yet effervescent Norwegian farmer's daughter. When I did, she smiled at me and said: "Sarah, I think what you're having is a faith crisis." Although she didn't intend it, her comment made me feel even more isolated.

When younger, I had pleaded with our reserved and tight-mouthed confirmation instructor at church to help me understand concepts like the holy spirit and the holy ghost. She got extremely flustered and angry. I'd been going to church for my entire life and still felt as if I just didn't get it. Nor were my parents ever able to explain their own faith to me in a way that I could understand. I once tried sharing my confusion and lack of faith in God with Mark's mom, but learned through her quick and surprised response that she would *never* question her faith—as if somehow even questioning it portended bad things. Though she meant no harm, I felt ashamed all over again for even mentioning it.

Thus, with my life in crisis, I learned that I just didn't seem to be capable of faith or a belief in God—at least not then. I wondered if I would ever find some sort of divine comfort for myself. All I knew was that you either believed or you didn't.

I just didn't.

CHAPTER 5

The Unraveling Begins

> Some people think that God is in the
> details, but I have come to believe that
> God is in the bathroom.
>
> Anne Lamott, *Plan B: Further
> Thoughts on Faith*

It was official. At thirty-six, after eleven years of, at times enthusiastic, fornication, the pink stripes lit up on the test strip. I was knocked up. We were already the fulfilled parents of our wonderful adopted children, George and Katherine, but the longing to experience a physical pregnancy had never left me. When I discovered I was pregnant, I was thrilled.

I'd been pregnant a half dozen times before, but, each time, it had ended in an early miscarriage. And in fact, this time my labs were once again discouraging, so I wasn't surprised when I was told to expect another miscarriage. I waited and grieved. The week before I was planning on going out of town, my gynecologist suggested a D&C so that I wouldn't have to endure going through a miscarriage on vacation.

While sitting in the waiting room to get my preparatory ultrasound, I did something weird. I put down the magazine I had been reading, closed my eyes, and prayed. "God, if you are there, please make this a real pregnancy, not just another miscarriage." Well, God didn't whisper in response, and no visions came. I felt nothing. When summoned, I walked into the ultrasound suite and lay down. And, low and behold, they detected a heartbeat. I was truly shocked, as was my doctor. The procedure was quickly called off, and I realized that I was officially eight weeks pregnant. That was a sweet surprise. For the first time in a long time, I felt gently optimistic. I wondered—had God actually responded to my prayer?

Months later, I found a huge, turn-of-the-century house in the classifieds—the same house in which I'd taken piano lessons at age nine from one of the kindest and most present adults I recall from my childhood. Could Mark and I make this place feel as warm and welcoming as she had? As we walked around with our Realtor, I could feel Mark jumping on board.

"I can see us here," he said, as he opened and closed a closet door. I could feel us invisibly coming together again. Mark was standing firmly alongside *us* instead of with his work, at least for the moment.

A few months later, I stood, hugely pregnant, in the driveway of our new home—a splendid, 6,500-square-foot, shake-shingled, Italianate colonial. The moving truck was being unloaded. I was experiencing more than a flicker of doubt—more like a full-on doubt tazer. With two small children and a third on the way, and two all-consuming careers, why had I taken on this enormous house? It meant much more space, more work, more—everything. To make life even more interesting, I was induced for delivery a few hours after the moving van left.

I took an all-too-brief six weeks of maternity leave, which I spent mostly "cluster feeding" our colicky newborn, Josephine. Cluster feeding (related to the incredibly useful noun clusterfuck) describes a situation when a baby seems to want to nurse for hours on end, leaving you wondering if she's not getting enough milk because you're a useless bunch of protoplasm not fit for lactation. I was already worried about my breasts because a plastic surgeon had once casually mentioned that I had "tubular breast deformity." (I had to look it up, too.) According to my research, it basically means having NG (*National Geographic*) boobs and pitiful milk production.

In every nonsuckling moment, I unpacked boxes and made plans for restoring our house

41

from top to bottom. Most people might have thought that the house was fine as it was, but I had a glorious vision of what was possible. I wanted to restore the gardens to their former glory. More than that, I longed for it to bring Mark and me close again, as so many previous projects had. We could be such a great team.

After Josephine's birth, Mark truly did cut back at work and started coming home earlier on a regular basis. But the new house hadn't helped to heal the marriage the way I had thought it might. The house was so big. What had we done?

I'd also developed severe and unrelenting undercarriage pain. I had a hunch that I had developed what's called post-partum rectal prolapse. I found myself mostly housebound, with my maternity leave almost over. When I caught myself fixating on the liquor cabinet, I booked an appointment for a surgical consultaion. I needed to self-administer an enema before I got there and explained to Mark that I needed him to take the kids for five minutes. I figured five minutes would be enough to get the deed done—at least the tricky part.

The need to devise a plan to give myself an enema made me realize how much our home life had become like a continual combat zone. "Mark, can you cover me? I'm going in!" Just as I began my "procedure," I heard the first security perimeter—our bedroom door—being breached. I brayed for Mark as loudly as I could, but to no avail. A few seconds later, the bathroom door flew open, and Buttercup (the pug), Katherine, and George all skidded into the bathroom on stockinged feet. They all stared at me lying on the floor with a combination of fascination and grave concern. Buttercup tilted her head, and Katherine asked, wide-eyed: "Mom, what you *doooing?*" As liquid began to trickle out below deck, I felt myself crumple further into the cold tile, feeling its chilling yet solid embrace. I stared back at them weakly, blinking. A few *very* tense seconds later, Mark arrived breathless, with Josephine in the crook of his arm, and hurriedly cleared the room. That's when I began to wonder what was happening to my life.

With the moving boxes mostly unpacked and my undercarriage pain resolved, I returned to work six weeks after Josephine's birth. By now, I had been in practice for six years since completing my five-year residency. So I was seasoned but exhausted.

One morning, after I had presented my cases at the weekly conference, a colleague came up to me and leaned in intimately. I figured he was going to congratulate me on our new baby or welcome me back to work. Instead, he kindly whispered: "Your zipper is totally undone on the back of your skirt." Mind you, he was reporting this to me *after* the conference was over, and I'd had my back to the room of mostly male colleagues for nearly the entire hour.

On another occasion—despite a sign on my closed office door that clearly read: "Do Not Enter"—a colleague inadvertently barged in on me while I was pumping breast milk at my desk. I sat helplessly in my chair, with both naked boobs solidly sucked into two transparent plastic horns, while a small motor quietly milked me. This normally shy gastroenterologist was so focused on his task that he actually sat down in the chair across from me and began rattling off patient findings and clinical hunches before he finally recognized that I was completely exposed. He blanched, apologized, and beat a hasty retreat.

A month later, I gave an encore zipper-down performance at another conference. This time, I didn't notice the problem until I was back at my office. I was unwittingly exposing myself on a regular basis. I finally gave up on street clothes altogether, opting instead for a uniform of zipperless blue surgical scrubs. My partners cocked their heads curiously at my new costume and asked whether I was covering surgery at the hospital. "No," I replied, "I'm just wearing scrubs to avoid ongoing indecent exposure."

And then there were the days when the kids were sick. Now that they were a tiny bit older, I tried sneaking George and Katherine into my office when they were too sick for school or daycare. I made a nest for them in my walk-in closet with a sleeping bag and a pillow so I could mother them, bringing them juice and hospital cafeteria donuts. I left the door slightly ajar and checked on them as often as I could. They seemed happy with the arrangement, and I felt lucky to be able to do this instead of medicating them and sending them to daycare as I had done during my residency. Most colleagues who entered my office never even noticed they were there. For this, I was grateful.

I wasn't able to conceal my identity as a mother completely, however. When I was at work, I thought about our kids in every available moment, imagining how they were spending their day. Was George behaving himself so his teacher wouldn't be so exasperated? Was Katherine's cold bothering her? She'd been coughing all night, and I hated to leave her in daycare feeling sick. I felt torn every single day—wanting to be a loving mother, wanting to be an outstanding physician. My colleagues who were fathers each had a great woman at home to hold down the fort so they could focus on work. I envied their apparent leisure and their ability to stay fully dressed at the office.

Josephine was a year old when another utterly irrational longing began tugging at me. I wanted a fourth child. Somehow, as crazy as things were, I didn't feel "done" yet. Mark balked at first, but slowly came around to the idea of adopting another child. Once we submitted our application, we were shown the paperwork and photos of Charlie, a child in Guatemala City who was being fostered by a faithful and loving woman while he awaited adoption. During the months while the legal process ground on, we received regular updates on his growth and development. Our approval seemed to be taking longer than usual to make its way through channels, however; so, in July, we all flew to Guatemala City to visit Charlie, now seven months old.

We were able have Charlie stay with us at our hotel for a few days, and we met his foster mom. We all snuggled him and got to know and love him. Weeks later, I flew down solo and brought Charlie, now eight months old, home to be a member of our family forever. I cannot defend my logic or explain it, but, after months of waiting, when Charlie arrived, our family felt complete.

Charlie possessed a calm serenity and was very affectionate. I wondered if it was just in him, or whether it was because he had spent his early months in such a nurturing foster family. They had given us a few dozen photos taken the night before he left the country. Each image featured a different child, teenager, or adult from his extended foster family standing in an open doorway holding Charlie in their arms with tears streaming down their faces. Some appeared devastated and others smiled bravely through their tears. Charlie smiled triumphantly in each picture. The first night he spent with us in Minnesota, he keened with terrible distress for hours until he collapsed and slept from sheer exhaustion. It seemed that being torn without warning from the familiar arms of those who had loved him had broken Charlie's heart.

Yet, despite this, he began to show us love. He so enjoyed snuggling, resting his head on our chests and softly reaching out his hands to be held by those he had decided to bless. When we ran into an old friend who had adopted children from Colombia, Charlie toddled over to him and reached out his arms. Gregg picked him up and smiled at him, then spontaneously burst into tears.

"This kid is really special, isn't he?"

"He is," I said, teary as well. "I swear he came into our family to teach us how to love."

Something in me shifted that day. I realized that I was longing to relish and enjoy our children— the magical and wondrous beings who'd come into our lives. I wanted to lavish them with love, bake for them, read to them, take them on adventures to the beach, to the movies, to the grocery store, and, above all, to be in their radiant presence.

CHAPTER 6

Breathing Lessons

The more relaxed you are, the better you
are at everything: the better you are with
your loved ones, the better you are with
your enemies, the better you are at your
job, the better you are with yourself.

Bill Murray, *New York Times*

My younger sister, Maria, had been clinically depressed on and off for years, so I have some understanding of depression. Her most recent hospitalization ultimately led to a diagnosis of Bipolar II, something my mother also suffered from briefly in later years. From what Maria told me and what I observed, being depressed was a crushing, disabling, and sometimes terrifying experience. Though I was definitely irritable, however, I didn't think that I was clinically depressed, so I considered other possibilities. Maybe I was trying to do too much. And yet, Mark and I were physicians with four kids. Didn't I *need* to be doing all this stuff?

Could I be depressed after all? Or manic?

What if I were diagnosed as being depressed and urged to take an antidepressant? At the time, half my family was on an antidepressant that had allegedly been responsible for sending one of my more distant relatives into a full-blown manic episode involving wigs, convertibles, and public nudity. I was having trouble staying fully dressed as it was. I worried what drugs like that might do to me.

When mental illness and addiction are a strong thread in your family, it's not uncommon to be haunted by the possibility that you, too, are on the verge of a mental breakdown or a dangerous dabbling of some kind. My awareness of my family history was good in some ways, because it kept me vigilant. But there was an anxiety that came with it. I stared into the mirror and wondered: *Could I slowly be going banana pancakes?*

During the approximately three minutes I could keep my eyes open before falling asleep each night, I had started skimming spiritually minded books by Deepak Chopra, Martha Beck, Marianne Williamson, and Louise Hay. What they were writing about seemed so "pie in the sky" to me. Thoughts become things. You can heal yourself. The entire Universe is inside you. Happiness is a choice. Have faith. In what? Could I even trust this stuff? While on vacation, I listened to an audiobook of Deepak Chopra's

Seven Spiritual Laws. Between the Sanskrit words and the foreign concepts, I could barely understand what he was getting at, but something in me desperately *wanted* to understand.

At this point, getting me off my prickly perch seemed an impossible task. I was confused as hell, overwhelmed, cranky, and I needed a little magic. Therapy just didn't appeal to me. But I'd been hearing about something new that intrigued me—life coaching. I was skeptical but also desperate. A Google search led me to a website run by a Canadian woman named Michele. In her headshot, she wore a warm smile and had nicely coiffed brown hair. On one of my precious days off, we did a free consultation call. She sounded so shockingly normal and kind on the phone that I signed up immediately for sessions three times a month.

I told no one about my life coach except Mark. Having a life coach seemed so horrifying to me. I'm a human being—wasn't I prepared for life by default? And I was having an awful time justifying the cost.

Michele and I talked for thirty minutes every other week on days I took off, while George was in school and Josephine and Katherine watched *Dora the Explorer* in the kitchen. It was an intense relief to pour out my thoughts and feelings to her—to speak to someone who would not judge me, who was neutral and safe. Even so, I frequently forgot our appointments. My life was so overbooked that I could barely remember what I was supposed to do next.

I shared with Michele what I couldn't tell anyone else about my life and my dysfunctional situation at work and at home. I told her that I worried I was asking too much of our kids by plucking them out of their beds in the early morning darkness to deposit them at daycare for nine and ten hours a day. They really had no choice. But didn't I have choices?

As I poured out my heart week after week, I began to feel better little by little. During these phone calls, it didn't seem as if much was happening. For the first few calls, Michele just listened. Then she began giving me little assignments. I experimented with her invitation to "minimize contact with cranky, unhappy people." Next, I slowly stopped spontaneously saying "yes" when my inner "nice girl" thought I should—like volunteering to take on extra cases at work when I was already busy. I also began taking my lunch breaks away from my desk whenever possible.

Gradually, over several weeks, I became more aware. I began noticing the number of mini-Snickers I ate at work. I noticed how often I was holding my breath. I found myself literally gasping for air in my office after unconsciously holding it for long periods. I began at least to acknowledge, with less guilt, that my life wasn't easy. I wasn't a failure, but I had a boatload on my plate.

I managed to find small ways to begin breathing again at work, and at home as well. At work, I practiced being extremely present—dealing with just one thing at a time so I could enjoy it rather than constantly multitasking. It helped. At home, I began making little découpage collages using glitter, glue, and antique images of cows. These excited me—perhaps because of a shared lactational vocation. I also became obsessed with finding Victorian images of bears, chickens, rabbits, and other animals. It seemed a little odd.

At night, after putting the kids to bed, I sat—exhausted, slumped over my glowing computer screen—poring over the images I'd started to collect, scanning them from vintage postcards. Anyone would have thought I was going mad. By 10:30, Mark was calling for me to come to bed as I intently studied a newly discovered Victorian rabbit in a blue-striped suit. These images delighted me, although I was unable to understand their purpose. But Michele confidently assured me: "If it makes you feel good, it's a good idea." Apparently, the more time I spent doing what I loved, the better.

The tiny worlds I was arranging and rearranging made up of wild creatures, insects, and flowers made me so happy inside. There was such exquisite beauty in each different species, from giraffe to caterpillar, and such mystery to the places where they lived—the ocean floor, the savannah, and the jungle. I loved layering them with beautiful colors and patterns to see the effect. Making—creating these worlds and giving them order—was just so deeply satisfying to me. Seeing a glass jar covered in delicate chartreuse tissue paper overlaid with a dark parrot tulip and a scarlet-winged butterfly made my heart leap with joy.

One morning, after signing in Josephine, Charlie, and Katherine at daycare's summer session with quick kisses and hugs, I barreled back down tree-lined streets toward our friends Maggie and David's house with George in the back seat. The morning had already been cringe-worthy. In my surgical scrubs, I had literally tackled George, then age eleven, in the yard back at home and physically wrestled him into the car. He didn't want to go to football camp. When I opened the car door at Maggie and David's, George promptly sprinted for cover across their large yard. I entered the house alone.

"Oh my lord, it's been a morning," I told Maggie and David. "George doesn't want to go to this camp."

David, who had a good eye for fugitives, pointed to a spot in the back yard where George was sporting a badly improvised fake limp to convince me that attending football camp with such a grievous injury wasn't even a remote possibility. David softly chuckled: "I think that means he *really* doesn't want to go."

Maggie's eighty-year-old mother, Lorraine, shrugged from the kitchen table and said dryly: "If he doesn't want to go, don't make him." That resonated. *A lot.* I began to feel a little more centered. "You're absolutely right, Lorraine. I think we're going to skip it for today. Thank you."

I dropped off George at his usual, nonfootball day camp. As I got back in my car, I wondered what parent in good conscience would ever force a kid to do something that terrified him. I discovered the answer to that question very quickly when Mark called to check in.

After decribing my brutal morning to him, I told him that I had decided to let George bag football camp and had dropped him off at his regular camp instead.

"You let him get away with that?" Mark asked, incredulous.

I immediately felt judged. My blood boiled. "If you're so disappointed in my performance, maybe you should leave work at noon and take George to football camp yourself."

"Fine," he replied. I could hear the quiet frustration in his voice. Great. I had just thrown an innocent eleven-year-old, terrified of getting beaten up at football camp, under the bus.

Later, when I paged Mark at the hospital, he reported that the lunchtime ambush had gone peacefully, in a tone that I can only describe as a tad smug. Apparently, George, whose behavior was a mystery to me at times, had not put up any fight at all. Maybe Mark had handled the situation with greater authority. Maggie's mom later confirmed the lack of struggle, saying that, when she picked him up from camp, George said: "I need to get to the mall tonight so my mom can buy me new football cleats." He apparently couldn't wait to go back for more.

But knowing that George enjoyed camp didn't assuage my anguish about how I had handled the situation. I apologized to both Mark and George. Then George and I talked about coming up with better ways to communicate the activities he did and didn't want to do. I didn't want to react like this anymore.

Clearly, here was another area of my life that was slipping out of control. I became more determined than ever to get myself to a place where I was more peaceful—a place where I could breathe.

CHAPTER 7

Sick Leave

I am not afraid of storms, for I am
learning how to sail my ship.

Louisa May Alcott, *Little Women*

One very sickly winter, a nasty crop of upper-respiratory illness and feverish crud swept through daycare and school. As the plague spread from child to child, Mark and I dealt with the situation in the least disruptive way we could—by taking turns staying home. It was becoming less practical and less satisfying to drag the kids to my office. And a few eyebrows had been raised when a sleeping bag was spotted in my closet.

Mark and I both worked for the same organization—a multispecialty practice of more than four hundred doctors—and we were both sensitive to the fact that our productivity was critical to our respective departments. On days when we split sick-kid duty, Mark canceled his morning patients and covered the shift at home; then I covered the afternoon, getting most of my cases finished in the morning so he could head to work.

In the previous six weeks, I'd had to miss six full or half days. Not great. Neither of us had access to advice on balancing childcare and work. We both worked solely with male colleagues who had wives taking care of business at home. All of the women staff physicians I had worked with during residency had full-time nannies holding down the home front. We'd tried that, hiring a nanny for a few months after Katherine came home, but it had ended in what felt like a disaster that involved filling out a police report. I filed that whole situation under *Nanny never again.*

I also still had flashbacks of dropping off our infant son, George, at the home of a near stranger in St. Paul—my daycare lady's "good friend"— on days when daycare was closed for illness or other reasons. Then, I felt that I had to do it just to survive. Now, I wanted to think of our children's needs first. It felt just awful to leave our kids with someone else when they were sick.

Physicians have no sick days, which I find ironic. We are supposed to use vacation days when ill, although the other pathologists in our group took sick days here and there and never counted them as vacation time. And I was almost never sick. That didn't seem fair either. But spring was coming, I told myself. This long bout of sickness couldn't last forever.

One day, while home caring for a sick child, I got an email about an emergency meeting in my department that had been scheduled for the next day. When I inquired what it was about, I discovered that, while I was out, my partners had called a meeting to discuss creating a new policy for "pathologists who stay home to care for sick children."

The implication seemed clear: I shouldn't be home caring for my sick kids. I ought to be able somehow to control my kids' illnesses; or worse, I was just a slacker. It suddenly felt to me as if the thousands of hours I'd poured into my work, including all the times I'd offered to help my partners, vaporized. I longed for my seven male partners to comprehend my situation.

I returned to the office the next day and sent out an email to my colleagues in which I gently, but firmly, suggested that the policy they were considering drafting was likely discriminatory. The original meeting was immediately canceled, and I was invited to a new, more intimate—and more threatening—meeting with my section chair and an upper-management person whom I'd never met.

When I told him about it, Mark was incensed. "But, that's just not right!" he said, shaking his head.

"We're trying as hard as we can here," I railed. "Kids get sick! I think they think I'm sitting home eating bon bons and watching *Scooby Doo* reruns! I wish you could come to this meeting with me. If they heard it from your viewpoint, it might be different." But I knew that would be ludicrous. In the 21st century, a woman doesn't bring her husband in to defend her at work.

Mark actually offered to come, but I told him I'd deal with it. Just before the dreaded meeting, I serendipitously ran into two women physician friends who were also moms. In a quiet back hallway of the main clinic, I confided in them about the proposed policy and imminent meeting. One of them, a typically proper, sweet, reserved being, gripped me by my shoulders, looked me dead in the eye, and growled ferociously: "Don't let those *motherfuckers* get you down. Don't let them!" The other, also instantly grave and serious, warned: "Whatever you do, don't let them see you cry." They were so fiercely kind and passionate that our brief encounter left me feeling stronger and more centered. It also made me wonder what soul-crushing scenarios they'd encountered as mothers in medicine.

Before going into the meeting, I ran up and down three or four flights of hospital stairs to ground myself, cued up my inner "Eye of the Tiger" soundtrack, and, as directed, strengthened my resolve not to cry. When I finally walked into the meeting, I felt strangely calm and collected.

I soon grasped that my fears about the proposed

policy were misdirected. My section chair and the management person actually didn't want to discuss the discriminatory policy they had proposed at all. Instead, they brought up things completely unrelated to the sick-child issue. Every time I tried to redirect the discussion, they sidestepped, calling into question my commitment to the job in general. Though they said it might not be relevant or even legitimate to bring up such things, they pointed out some raw quality-control data that hadn't yet been fully analyzed to put into question my competency. The data, on further analysis, actually supported my excellence as a diagnostician.

Now, errors are part of the job in medicine, and we all knew it. And I had long ago forged a direct correlation in my brain between my level of stress and the quality of my work. So I knew that I was not immune to errors. But then their comments became even *more* personal. I was questioned about the time I spent on the phone and challenged about how I spent my downtime, completely disregarding the fact that other partners played online games during the day between cases or left to go swimming in the afternoon or eat donuts and drink coffee in the lounge. I was definitely feeling bullied.

Then the management person, who was taking it all in, asked me: "Sarah, why don't you just go part time?"

The offer seemed patronizing to me in the moment. I knew that, if I went to part-time status, I'd be treated differently from my partners. And having to fight for my own salary, rights, and benefits seemed like the last thing I'd want to do. Besides, "going part time" was incredibly *off topic.* Switching to part-time status wouldn't solve the problem of caring for sick kids. Kids don't get sick only on scheduled days off. But I knew that becoming emotional, trying to fight back, or starting an argument wasn't going to help the situation. So I calmly explained my position.

"I don't know how part-time status would change my having to stay home to care for my sick kids," I told them. "Besides, as you know, I'd be completely alone to bargain for myself if I got separated from the group like that. Right now that doesn't sound very appealing."

By the time the meeting ended, no decisions had been made, no ultimatums given. I felt that at least I had stood proudly on my own side and spoken up for myself.

At home, just before falling asleep, my anger began to subside as I sensed that my section chair was stuck as well. He had to run the department and answer to the partners, who, I presumed, were complaining about my periodic parental absences. The next morning, as I pulled my car into a space in the underground lot at work, I felt calm. I walked slowly to my office. Something inside me had resolved to care less about the politics at work and more about what was happening to my life. I was beginning to think this situation might, in fact, be helped by asking myself: "How can I create the kind of life I want for myself and my family?"

Before the day's cases started to land on my desk, my section chair came into my office and shut the door. "You know, Sarah," he began, "after going home, I thought about our meeting, and I need to say that I'm really sorry about the whole conversation yesterday. Our approach was wrong. We just weren't being fair. I apologize. Moving forward, there will be no new policy."

I was bowled over. I thanked him and grinned, saying: "Here's to a spring of healthy kids!" I wasn't sure what had shifted overnight, but I was deeply grateful for this honest human moment. It felt like grace.

As if their immune systems suddenly grew hale overnight, our kids weren't sick one additional day in the spring months following the meeting. A few weeks later, however, one of my partners was hospitalized for an unexpected illness and was out of the office for two weeks—ten working days, nearly twice the number I'd missed caring for our sick children. We all cheerfully rallied to cover for him. No emergency meetings were called. He returned to work, healthy again. Nothing was said. But I doubt that I was the only one to see the irony. If we couldn't cover for each other and care about each other's lives, then what had we become?

CHAPTER 8

Feeding the Bears

I hope you live a life you're proud of. If
you find that you are not, I hope you find
the strength to start all over again.

Eric Roth, *The Curious Case
of Benjamin Button*

As I detached more and more from office
politics, and the whole sick-kid incident
faded, I began to dream a new dream: I wanted
to work less. How could I do that? My coach
Michele encouraged me to "act as if" I were
making only 80 percent of my income and see
how that suited me. While it had irritated me like
hell to have part-time employment suggested to
me as an option during the infamous sick-kid
meeting, I had to admit that the irritation had
arisen partly because I knew that it might not be
a bad option.

I didn't know a lot of physicians who worked
less than full time, and I knew that many old-
school physicians frowned on it. In my teens,
when I asked my father about another woman

physician in town who worked only three days a week and seemed to have a great family life, he said: "You know what they say—part-time doctor, part-time brain." Then he laughed haughtily, reflecting the deeply held idea that medicine requires you to surrender everything to achieve excellence. He might feel differently now, but his words still clanged in my head.

My father was entirely devoted to his practice and his research projects. When he wasn't at his clinic running from room to room seeing patients or playing with us at home, he was in his study, reviewing research data from his projects or reading journals. He was a devoted father *and* a dedicated physician. With my mom mostly at home, he was able to do both with ease. His father was a psychiatrist in New York City, and his grandfather had been a general practitioner before him. I came from a solid line of caring and hardworking men of medicine—none of whom had ever faced my maternal dilemma.

Despite my worries that part-time practice might mean a practice that was somehow diminished, I persevered. By examining our finances, I quickly saw how we could live on less—fewer fancy vacations and more frugal shopping. A few months later, I boldly requested part-time status and my request for a 90 percent position was granted. This meant that I would have one regular day off every other week. In the years that followed, I slowly began to ratchet back my work at the hospital—90 percent, then 80 percent, and eventually 60 percent. Finally, I had more time to breathe.

Around this time, I had a vivid, frightening dream. There were three enormous, story-high grizzlies in the back yard. I was inside the house with my kids, family, and friends. The monstrous bears were menacingly tossing around huge propane tanks. They were pissed off. In the dream, I was terrified for all of us, especially for the kids, who were peeking curiously out the basement window at the giant bears. But the kids weren't afraid at all. All the other adults were upstairs drinking wine and having a party, so I ran up to warn them. They weren't even remotely interested either. I had the sense that I was on my own to deal with these beasts.

According to Jung, dreams are meant to help you guide your waking self into wholeness and even offer solutions to the difficulties you're facing. I broke down the dream into symbols and tried to determine what message each had for me—for Sarah, the dreamer. As I did this, I discovered that the bears were angry simply because they were *hungry*. They were starving, actually. I realized that the bears represented my creativity, and suddenly knew that I needed to feed my starving bears. I knew I had to further lighten my load.

• • •

Throughout my childhood, my parents had owned a cabin on Lake Pequaywan. I grew up spending nearly every weekend of my childhood there, and it held a lot of special memories for me. When my parents announced that they were selling it and planned to build a year-round home right next door, Mark and I had mixed feelings. We knew they wanted us to buy the cabin. We didn't feel ready for it, but we feared the opportunity would be gone if we didn't say yes immediately. We trusted that it would be a good thing and bought it.

Now, as I began thinking about how to lighten my workload, I realized that packing up the minivan with bag upon bag of groceries on a Friday night after a long work week to go to the cabin wasn't really working for me. Add the perils of open water—and the hyper-vigilance it required when toddlers were around it—to the work of maintaining a whole additional home, and it was clear that something had to give.

My parents had built right next door. I *loved* the fleeting moments of dog-paddling in the lake with my mom, watching my dad explain where the frogs were hiding in the pond to my son, and just being there with my parents. But getting to the cabin and maintaining it took more than we had to give. The Sunday clean-up and packing often started at 8:00 in the morning and ran all the way into Monday. We mopped, washed clothes, put away life jackets, and emptied the fridge. And it started all over again when we landed at home with our laundry and left-over groceries.

Though it dismayed my mom, we decided that selling the cabin would definitely lighten our load. It was probably one of the first times I ever did something as a full-fledged adult that truly upset my mother. It wasn't easy to stand in our truth, but it felt so liberating once we did.

The day we closed on the cabin sale, I felt inspired to inquire about downsizing possibilities for our home in town. Working part-time really appealed to me and a smaller mortgage would certainly make that easier. We'd have less to clean and maintain, and it would force us to be leaner with our possessions. Our Realtor told us about a much smaller home priced at a third the value of our current house. It was a newer, one-level home built on slab, with a nice bedroom and bath for Mark and I that seemed like a perfect haven.

Mark was happy with the possibility of not having to put up as many storm windows every fall and impressed with how much lower our energy bills would be. I was excited by the prospect of the increased closeness that the new great room would make possible. We decided together that it would feel really good to simplify everything—from the size of our house to the size of our mortgage.

We made an offer and put our Italianate manse on the market. We got an almost immediate full-price offer—and the next day, the stock market crashed. Our buyers disappeared into thin air. It took longer to sell the house than we had expected—seven very long months, in fact. I wondered if I'd made a mistake in longing for this change. What if we were stuck with two houses for years? Each morning, I did affirmations from my stack of self-help books—"I'm leaning into the benevolence of the Universe" was my favorite—and no matter how down I felt, it always helped. In the end, we found wonderful buyers and decamped with half of our possessions to our more modest home.

The older kids grumbled for several months about the move, complaining about missing things like the pool table and the ability to entertain an almost unlimited number of friends all the time. They'd become attached to the old place and the freedom, maybe even the prestige, it offered. But I told them that, when they were old enough, they could decide for themselves where and how they wanted to live.

As we downsized, I sometimes got the sense from the bewildered stares people gave us that they thought we were in dire financial straits. Some asked how we could leave the big house so soon after completing a sky's-the-limit kitchen remodeling. And in fact, the kitchen was amazing; it had been a great experience co-creating it. It wasn't until after we'd finished it, however, that we found that what we craved was not the marble countertops, fancy appliances, and French chandelier. It was freedom.

We kept all of our most treasured belongings and placed the rest in an estate sale that was run by a friend in the antique business. At the sale, one of my colleague's wives stood by my side, staring at the sea of beautiful things—everything from Spode china to hand-hooked rugs to gilded mirrors—and asked me if I was going to miss it all. When I grinned and answered, "No, not really," she seemed surprised and almost disappointed. The only things I truly regretted selling were a few spools of ribbon, which I promptly repurchased. When the sale was over, I could already feel a new, simpler way of living trying to take root.

I learned that our house needed to shrink so we could grow. I sensed that, by ridding myself of excess baggage, I could get closer to what really mattered. The physically exhausting process of downsizing galvanized an important lesson for me: Every object you take on board must be dealt with—eventually.

CHAPTER 9

Needle in a Haystack

It doesn't matter who you are or what you look like, so long as somebody loves you.

Roald Dahl, *The Witches*

Pathology is basically a profession in which you often find yourself searching for a needle in a haystack. Learning to recognize patterns that lead to accurate diagnoses can be a little like playing *Where's Waldo*, where Waldo is a malignant cell or a specific disease profile. I'd relished my work in pathology for nearly two decades, but when I started to find it less and less fascinating, it began to worry me. I was learning to enjoy my current life much more by shifting my perspective and finding ways to do more things that felt good. Now, what I was really longing for was a whole new kind of work. The field that had once felt like a shelter from the storm was beginning to feel less cozy to me.

I considered practical options for fixing my current predicament. I was only in my early forties; perhaps I could do another fellowship and

71

become Board certified in a new subspecialty. When Mark had yearned for new challenges, he had trained to be a spine interventionalist and collected a second certification in pain medicine, a great move for him. I thought that perhaps developing a new subspecialty might make both financial and professional sense for me as well.

The only pesky problem was that I was loving my vintage images of octopuses and horses, my glitter, and my handwritten letters from turn-of-the-century Paris. I wasn't exactly yearning for a fellowship in, say, gastrointestinal pathology. I had also noticed that my passion was shifting from discovering what caused disease toward discovering what creates health. I was coming to realize that our whole medical system was focused on what was *wrong* rather than on what could be *right*.

In multidisciplinary conferences, for instance, I found that I was more interested in the status of a patient's spirit than in quibbling over cellular details or genetic test results. I started asking questions that other physicians, in their role as "disease eradicators," were less interested in addressing. I was becoming much more curious about the issues that social workers and nurses brought up: What is a patient's support system like? Does the patient feel loved? What other stressors are present outside the patient's medical situation? I began to ask myself questions like:

What might have happened if we'd intervened a long time ago and helped this person find love, connection, and a supportive community? Would that patient still be ill now?

In pathology, we operated at the point where disease has already manifested. I longed to work from a place farther *upstream,* to see how much disease we could avoid (or delay for decades) if we worked at the level of spirit. How could we prevent the disease from assembling itself? I worried about whether these strange desires and questions made me selfish and self-absorbed. And I wondered whether medicine was missing something *big.* While I acknowledged that allopathic (traditional Western) medicine was still clearly needed, I began to suspect that spirit must also be cared for and nurtured. Without tending to the spirit, we can't hope to create health.

One afternoon, while sitting at my desk, which was piled high with cases awaiting finalization, I noticed how low I was still feeling. Working with my coach, Michele, had helped me realize that my circumstances and colleagues were not the problem—that finding my "feel good" was an inside job. I was a lot less frazzled. But I had also realized that the place I was in didn't feel comfortable anymore. How was I ever going to figure out what I was supposed to be doing?

Later that day, I went onto the Internet in search of some sort of salve for my soul and stumbled onto a Rascal Flatts video. Country music isn't really my jam, so I'll never be sure what made me click "play." But when I began to listen to "My Wish," I burst into tears.

The warm voice singing the song struck a resounding chord inside me; my whole being resonated with its message. The lyric expressed a hope that everything would be okay for me in my life—even if it seemed, currently, as though all the doors were closed. It encouraged me to find my way to a "window" again. It told me that I was loved. My eyes filled and tears washed down my cheeks in recognition. This was *my* wish as well—for me and for everyone. In fact, *it was my prayer.*

That night, while whipping up some bison spaghetti (because they couldn't be factory farmed, and I didn't want to inflict any more suffering) and sipping a glass of boxed red wine, I forced my kids to listen to the song. I played it loudly, over and over. "Isn't this song awesome?" I broadcast to no one in particular. Katherine generously offered: "It's pretty good, Mom; I like country music." Josephine shrugged, as if to say: I'm giving you a pass here, but don't push your luck. Charlie ran over, threw his arms around my waist, hugged me for a long time, and said: "I like it, Mom." George, now fourteen, wandered by and cocked his head, surprised at the sudden appearance of country music in my repertoire.

"It's my new jam," I offered to him. He looked a little curious, then nodded upward with his chin in mild approval.

I knew the kids were just indulging me. They seemed somehow to know that I needed this schmaltzy country song right now. But I knew—at some very deep level—that I had stumbled upon the precious needle in my own haystack.

CHAPTER 10

Radical Sabbatical

Enlightenment always tastes of freedom.

Martha N. Beck, *Steering by Starlight*

Three months. That's what I asked from my section chair. Three months completely away from my pathology duties. I was already part-time, working just a couple of days a week. I was curious what might grow in my life if I dropped just one of the "part-times" that crowded my resumé. He readily agreed. I think the wise and kind secretaries at the hospital suspected just how life-altering my sabbatical would be, however. When I left at the end of June, they threw me a party.

During my sabbatical, I immersed myself in Martha Beck's life-coach training program a few days a week. Learning virtually alongside fifty other like-minded women (and a few men) was heaven. I felt *much* less alone. I had learned about Martha's training program after I took a weekend life-coaching telecourse that Michele had suggested. I liked coaching my practice clients, and I wanted to know more. When I dialed in to a call from Martha for prospective students, I was sold.

After telling us that she had lived all her life with ADD (Attention Deficit Disorder)—"my brain is like a squirrel on meth and that's why the CEO of Martha Beck, Inc. is here with me today"—she got right to the point. "If you really want to learn how to coach people," she said, "you've come to the right place. Even if you don't know why you're here, you've come to the right place." I was amazed that this Harvard-educated writer had just admitted in public that she had ADD. Was she joking? I couldn't even tell, but I found that I really didn't care, because I sensed that this authentic woman and her team could help me have *fun* while walking this new unknown path.

Martha's band of coach trainees were smart, sensitive, and down to earth. We'd all been undergoing huge meltdowns in our respective lives—divorces, cancer diagnoses, careers dead-ending, recovery from addiction, crippling grief, mysterious illnesses, kids leaving the nest—yet we all shared a common desire. We wanted to help people who were suffering. Before we could help others, however, we first needed to sort ourselves out.

During my sabbatical, I was thrilled to be home so that I could finally be a mom who was actually present, both literally and figuratively. Ironically, not all of the kids were so sure they liked this new arrangement—especially George. Now I was home. *A lot.* Still suspicious and slightly shell-shocked from the whole downsizing experience, George eyed me warily. He repeatedly asked me: "When are you going to go back to your *real* job? Life coaching isn't a real job." I think he was reading my mind, because I was wondering the exact same thing. The kids had picked up a fair amount of money anxiety from me when we downsized, and now they were aware that I wasn't making much money anymore.

Watching YouTube one night, I cringed at Cheri O'Teri's satirical *Saturday Night Live* portrayal of "Liza Life Coach," a perky and overzealous airhead who was clearly in need of more coaching than her clients. But this wasn't real coaching, I protested. Coaching meant helping clients find their own way, not ordering them around. It seemed, however, that life coaching had all the cachet of selling snake oil. Even my mother went out of her way to mention (in hushed tones) that a friend from college trained to be a life coach, but had never attracted enough clients to make a living at it.

All these changes I was making did, in fact, feel precarious, and somehow George's lack of confidence in me was especially disturbing. I tried to laugh it off and reassure him that all would be well. I was trusting that the Universe was benevolent—and I hoped I was right.

I needed more practice coaching clients, so I offered coaching to our kids (with a cash incentive!) so I could try my skills on them. George was skeptical at first, but came around when he realized he could earn twenty dollars and after I assured him that I had no hidden agenda.

I let George guide his own session by asking him to think of one thing he had to do that week that he didn't want to do. He picked disciplining Josephine, his younger sister. He had recently taken it upon himself (without our encouragement) to step in when Josephine was really angry. Lately, she'd had a few tantrums and occasionally had thrown things at people in anger. As we dove deeper into the subject, I asked him: "Why do you believe you need to discipline Josephine? You're not the parent."

Finally, he confessed. "If I don't step in and stop her now from doing bad stuff, she could end up in jail later, or get in big trouble at some point in her life."

Suddenly I had a significant new insight into why George was sometimes so hard on Josephine. Deep down, he loved her and cared about her, and was seriously worried that she'd end up in jail if he didn't put a stop to her behavior.

Days later, Josephine got angry and threw a

portable phone in a huff over a perceived slight. George began to charge after her. "George!" I shouted. "*Stop now!* Not your job. I'm the mom. I've got this." He stopped and shrugged his shoulders. I allowed Josephine to calm down in her room for a while before I knocked on the door to talk with her. And this time, I wasn't as frustrated with George. I could see that what he was doing stemmed from love and concern.

George wasn't the only volunteer from whom I learned a lot. Charlie, our scarlet macaw—uber-affectionate, charming, and prone to loud squawking at times—asked to be coached on the thing he hated doing most: brushing his teeth. When I probed deeper into what might happen if he skipped brushing his teeth, I discovered something very revealing.

"If I don't brush my teeth, I'll get in trouble," he told me.

"So what; you've gotten into trouble before," I prodded. "Why would that be so bad?"

"Because I might have to make all the beds."

"Well, you've had to make beds before. Who cares? Why would that be so bad?"

Charlie looked concerned. "Because if I couldn't do it, I might get sick and throw up and then it would be a mess."

"Okay. So you've made messes before. Why would that be so terrible?"

"Because then I might have to leave this family and go live with a different one."

Incredible! I suddenly understood. Refusing to brush his teeth was linked deeply to his adoptee fear of being abandoned by our family. Suddenly, as I replayed all his fits at bedtime about brushing his teeth, I got it. This wasn't about finding the perfect SpongeBob toothpaste to inspire him to brush. He just needed reassurance that his place in this family was permanent. When I told him that, no matter what ever happened, he would *always* be our son and that he would also always have his birth family, he leaned in for a hug. Mark and I continued to reassure him all summer and, sure enough, the bedtime tantrums around brushing lessened dramatically.

I still worried, however, that George was right—that choosing a career as a life coach would be professional and social suicide. After my experiences with him and Charlie, however, I wasn't about to quit.

At first, three months of sabbatical freedom felt like an *enormous* amount of time to me. And, for once, my time wasn't consumed by caring for an infant. I planned to use the time to focus on learning more about coaching. Inspired by my earlier interest in découpage, I also hoped to do more work with my BFF Suzi, with whom I shared a passion for interior design.

I was forty-two and, for the first time since I was fifteen, my sabbatical afforded me the rare gift of some unplanned free time. And it was summer—when happy, well-groomed, organized families leapt off docks into lakes, traveled harmoniously, planted gardens, set up lemonade stands, and went to the beach. Until this point, I hadn't been able to do many of these things with my kids, except on scheduled vacations. Now they could finally sleep in. So could I. I welcomed this strange new leisure.

Not so fast, missy.

My mother called the house in early July to ask what exactly I planned to accomplish on my sabbatical, warning that I'd better set some clear goals or I might be disappointed. I suppressed a sigh, and tried to explain that all I'd ever done was work and accomplish things. Couldn't I just rest for a while? Her response was to warn me how quickly the time I had would fly by.

I felt defeated that even my own mother didn't really approve of me taking a complete break. It also annoyed me. Yet, I sensed she was right. But what else was I supposed to be *doing?* I had quite a bit going on with life-coach training and part-time design work with Suzi. Couldn't I just *be?*

That summer, the days passed gloriously slowly, as if the Universe had held all of those sunny days when I was working in the hospital in escrow and delivered them to me in a grand payout—one big, warm, cloudless day after another. I relished each day, each breeze. Our neighbors probably thought I was nuts—standing at the bottom of the driveway, admiring the kids' chalk art and exclaiming over the beauty of the day. It was as if I had been born again—not in a Pat Robertson way but organically. As if a long-lost part of me were waking up and coming to life.

For the first time, I was able to offer rides to other kids to and from soccer. I could begin to repay all the favors I'd received from others. This felt deeply satisfying. I suddenly understood that, when other moms had helped me out in the past, saying "no problem" or "my pleasure," *they really meant it*. I drove to several of George's games in Minneapolis with a carload of teenaged boys, and it was such fun to listen to their banter and hear them belting out "All the Single Ladies" at the top of their lungs in a newly achieved lower register.

On other days, we just went exploring like life pirates. One day, I took the three younger kids to a place just up the north shore of Lake Superior—a sort of rabbit-and-llama petting zoo coupled with odd logging-camp paraphernalia, including large papier-mâché loggers posed in funky logging-camp scenes. It was endless fun to watch them feed the critters, and the trading post had rock candy, agates, and jackalopes. It was the kind of aimless, imaginative, idling time for which we had all been longing.

There were also dark days when I was overwhelmed with learning about coaching, keeping the house neat enough to live in, and trying to navigate the many locations for weekly soccer games, practices, and skill sessions for Katherine and George. My brain struggled to keep all these details straight. All I ever wanted to be was home and now that I was, why was it so incredibly hard?

Between soccer games, design work with Suzi, and coach-training calls, I had a little surplus time in the early morning and late afternoon when the kids were either sleeping or otherwise entertained. I began to wander outside with Buttercup, our pug. I never realized how Nature-starved I had been until now. I walked to the edge of the woods near our house and stood there, looking into the shady darkness. In the stillness, I could sense a great buzzing energy, but I wasn't quite ready to find out what it was. Instead of going into the dark woods, I hung out in the cattails at the marsh near the edges of the woods with a bunch of red-winged blackbirds, who really were excellent company.

The marsh really began to work on me. I felt softer there, more peaceful and more myself. One day, while sitting in the grass watching the cattails bend and blow, I felt as if the wind were trying to talk to me as it softly bent the tall stalks. It was as if we were conversing—the wind speaking and I listening—although nothing specific was being said. I was just suddenly *aware*. I began to get the feeling—to know—that *everything in Nature is alive and can speak to me*. I grabbed a few minutes of video of the scene on my phone, because I didn't want to forget it. It was comforting and also exhilarating. I wanted to know what to do about this new ability to commune with Nature; I wanted to learn more about this peculiar mode of communication.

Eventually, as the weeks rolled by, I began to wander deeper into the woods. And they began to speak to me and reveal things in their own wild way. One cold fall day, it felt as if everything were being laid bare—as if everything were full of truth. The leaves had fallen away and the grasses had withered to the ground. The chickadees were singing out their own honest cries: "Sweetie, sweetie."

As I witnessed the pure honesty of the wild, my own untruths became more apparent to me. I needed to ask clearly for what I needed. I needed to become quiet so that I could hear. A large dead tree whose arms extended in all directions seemed to be pointing me home. A huge old pine with a mossy two-part trunk drew me in, and I began to notice that it looked like a lady buried upside down, with just her hips and legs left above ground. I became acutely aware of the season—how, as fall marched on, it became eerily silent and all the energy seemed to go underground. Faces appeared to me everywhere—in rocks and in tree trunks—and they all seemed to have different personalities and feelings. I couldn't recall ever being so aware that everything was so alive *and that it was also aware of me.*

It was at this point that I had my second significant dream about animals, this one sweet. There were beautiful beluga whales nuzzling my fingers as I sat at the back of a boat. The boat was riding very low in the water and so it was a bit precarious, but the sea was calm and gentle. The message from the whales was simple:

Everything looks good. Just *slow down* so we can communicate with you. And try to float a little higher.

CHAPTER 11

Slam-Dunk Diagnosis

"You're mad, bonkers, completely off
your head. But I'll tell you a secret.
All the best people are."

Lewis Carroll, *Alice in Wonderland*

I made a significant discovery while on
sabbatical. With some distance, I was able
to see that, in many ways, I had always been
different from other physicians. They seemed
satisfied with *medicine for life*—or at least they
had surrendered to the prospect. They seemed
practical. Or maybe resigned. Some didn't
have kids, so they were more free to commit to
medicine while also pursuing parallel dreams—
like playing in a metal band, rescuing injured
hawks, or studying Lithuanian cuisine. I, on
the other hand, had *many* different desires, and
I wanted to do them *all*. Being sentenced to
pathology for life now felt incredibly stifling.

Being away from the office also gave me a new
perspective. I began to notice that I'd developed
a certain toughness in medicine that wasn't in my

nature. Even the metaphors used in my daily work seemed masculine and violent. When we made a difficult diagnosis—for example, one resulting in a partial brain resection—we said: "We pulled the trigger." I now realized that I had allowed the field of medicine—where competition and criticism are often fostered—to squelch my own softness. In response, I had found solace among the nurturing women in my immediate work environment—the secretaries and technicians. Without their laughter and encouragement, I would truly have been miserable at work. With them, I noticed that I could be myself in a way that I couldn't with my male physician partners.

I made another connection after a couple of women acquaintances confessed that they had recently both been diagnosed with ADD. One was a physician like me; the other was a professional design consultant. I could relate to a lot of things about the consultant. She was off-the-wall funny and prone to blurting out whatever was on her mind, sometimes with mixed responses from her audience. A bit of a loose cannon, irrepressible. Hmm. That sounded familiar.

Intrigued by these encounters, and curious as to why I was struggling so much with being at home with the kids over the summer, I decided to learn more about ADD, going about it in the same way I tackled all problems—by reading lots of books and asking lots of questions. I devoured

Driven to Distraction by Edward Hallowell and John Ratey, and recognized myself on nearly every page. I could see the part of me that wanted to categorize a pathology case but wasn't interested in "super-sub-sub-categorizing" it. I'm decidedly a lumper, not a splitter, which had been distressing when working with people who relished hairsplitting. For example, I found it frustrating when a colleague felt the need to run dozens of expensive and highly detailed tests to further categorize an aggressive tumor in an elderly patient who couldn't possibly undergo the chemoptherapy that would be required to treat it. I favored being practical rather than splitting hairs simply because we could. Moreover, my mentors at the county hospital where I was trained had taught me that every dollar should be spent to its best effect.

I also recognized that I worked best in the quiet of my tomb-like office with the door closed. Overstimulating, noisy, or cluttered environments (like parts of our house) confounded me. I recognized my "let's cut to the chase" tendency—an aversion to taking in too much information—and my impulsive desire for speedy conclusions. All these traits often characterize people with ADD. They can also be a strength, of course. But I began to see how they often sabotaged my relationship with Mark and my family. And I recognized that I often felt as if I were in a hurry, as if I were in a big race. But a race to where?

In fact, I put a mental check mark next to nearly every ADD symptom the authors mentioned. After finishing the book, I felt discouraged and even more confused. *Could I really have ADD?* If so, why hadn't it been recognized earlier—in elementary school? After all, I'd made it through all those years of schooling, including medical school, and no one had ever suggested something might be different about me in this way. I'd flourished in my professional career—at least up until now. But then I realized that, before leaving on sabbatical, I'd been finding it harder than ever to sit at my microscope.

I decided to see a well-respected local psychologist and have an evaluation done that involved testing and a lengthy personal interview. After an hour of exploratory questions, the psychologist suggested that I might have mild anxiety and perhaps a bit of a "caustic personality" (say what?). I was told to return to his office; he needed to administer some tests.

A week later, I took the computerized TOVA screening (Test of Variables of Attention) after a big old mocha from Starbucks. I thought I was slaying it. When the test was reviewed, however, my diagnosis was a slam dunk. My ability to attend to incredibly boring stimuli for long periods of time was, as Martha Beck had once so aptly described it, akin to that of a demented squirrel on meth. According to the psychologist, my ADD had probably gone unnoticed because, when I was a kid, ADD was a disease generally attributed to boys, and because I probably had an inherent IQ high enough to override most of my cognitive challenges. So when I worked really hard, I could compensate for my deficits. This made sense to me.

This diagnosis led me deeper into myself. I began to explore how it had affected me and my life. The more I learned about it, the more I started to understand why certain things were immensely challenging for me. Even typing an email in our noisy house could send my brain into overload. Watching a film about Temple Grandin's life was an epiphany for me. When Temple, diagnosed with autism in elementary school, went away to college, the noise and environment were so incredibly overstimulating that she had to find a way to calm herself. She'd observed that cattle became docile after entering the "squeeze chute" used to hold them still for vaccination and branding. So she designed and built a little "squeeze chute" in her dorm room that effectively held her and calmed her. She called it her "gentling contraption."

I totally *got* how Temple Grandin felt in over-stimulating situations. I desperately needed a gentling contraption of my own, or at least air-traffic-controller earmuffs—something to help me during times of loudness and distress. I began to make connections between autism and ADD, especially the inattentive kind of ADD I suspected I had. People with these characteristics tended to spend more time in the theta-brainwave state characteristic of daydreaming, one of my favorite pastimes.

I also began to understand how I could get so much done in a very short time at work. I was in ADD *hyperfocus* mode, which allowed me to tune out the world and tune in to the task at hand. However, any distractions while I was in hyperfocus mode were irritating as hell to me.

It was also my ADD that apparently gave me the tendency to blurt out whatever was on my mind. A few painful "unfiltered Sarah" moments came flooding back to me with a new understanding. Like the time when I was nine and told my favorite teacher to "go to hell!" when he wouldn't let me sit out a game of dodgeball where it seemed as if the balls were constantly bombarding me. Or the time when I locked my least favorite babysitter in our bathroom until my mom got home because I was sick of her being in charge. Or all those times that I impulsively told my mother to "fuck off," even though I knew it would get me grounded. Stealing liquor from parents, buying an ounce of pot and spending a summer smoking it with a friend. Doing tequila shots while driving around on the first night I had my driver's license. Brashly getting high in the stadium bathroom before football games while I was on the cheering squad. Telling a friend who told me she wanted to have another baby and seemed confused about how to go about it: "Why don't you just go home and have Roger stick it in there tonight?" The list goes on.

Okay, sure, I sometimes blurted things out and could be impulsive. What I let slip might not always have seemed empathetic. Or appropriate. Or polite. Or even okay. But I reminded myself that I was also valued on the foundation board on which I served because I had no problem addressing the elephant in the room when other people were afraid to speak up. My nonfiltering self was sometimes an advantage. *I wasn't a bad person.* I was honest—to a fault. And tender. I often burst into tears when I sensed the pain of another being.

So I spent a few months grieving for my inner little Sarah who'd worked so hard and tried to fit in. And then I began to claim my own status as a creative being. I remembered Walt Whitman's words: "I am large. I contain multitudes." I suddenly realized that I was here to use my own strange multitudes to bring balance to the world. I began seeing this freakiness, this strange irrepressibility, everywhere. But I began to look beyond its drawbacks, and to see the *beauty* it could bring.

I began to expand my understanding to include other groups as well—addicts and those with depression or anxiety. I suspected that just about everybody with this type of disorder was here, not to be fixed but to learn to express themselves and (with help) find their own way.

I began to ask myself: What if we could love, accept, and circle the wagons around these folks, as I'd experienced in my own life? Then perhaps even more good could unfold.

PART TWO

Heeding the Call

"You've got to be able to make those daring leaps or you're nowhere," said Muskrat.

Russel Hoban, *The Mouse and His Child*

CHAPTER 12

Throwing Bones

"I think it will come true," said Mother,
"because it is a special kind of good wish
that can make itself come true."

Russel Hoban, *A Birthday for Frances*

I was sitting at my parents' cabin when my phone buzzed. It was Suzi, asking if I wanted to go to South Africa with her. Her cousin Brian, who worked there, was planning to marry a girl whose family lived in a remote village. He needed a family delegation to attend the *lobola*, or bride-price negotiation.

Strangely enough, six months earlier, Suzi and I had declared that we both wanted to go to South Africa. It had just sounded intriguing. But the possibility felt even more significant now, because it would allow me to deepen my study of wild animals.

Since my experience in the marsh, and through the animals showing up in my dreams, I'd stumbled deep into the idea of animal wisdom— that animals somehow have helpful messages they can convey to humans. I was reading every book on animal totems and shamanism I could find. My first introduction to the concept had come from Ted Andrews's book *Animal Speak*, which I picked up in a New Age store when we were on vacation one weekend. Because I was on sabbatical, I felt more relaxed—more open than usual and freer to explore new ideas. The store itself drew me in, and I didn't want to leave when it was time to go. It was stuffed with crystals, books, chakra charts, and statues of deities. I couldn't get enough of the atmosphere. It felt so good to me.

From Andrews's book, I learned that the power of totems is based in the belief that any and all wild animals that cross your path come bearing helpful messages. When you can decipher them, you have an easier time navigating life. *I was fascinated.* After reading the book, I decided to share what I was learning on Facebook. I asked if anybody wanted to know what a certain animal totem meant. I must have had fifty people comment, curious about what certain animals symbolized. The experience of conversing online with these people thrilled me. I wasn't alone. This seemed to be a clue for me. In a game of "Colder, Hotter," I was *getting warmer*.

As I began to observe the wild animals that crossed my path and search for their visits' meanings, I slowly started to internalize the ancient belief that *everything that is, is alive and can speak to you.* I began to notice creatures everywhere, and each one seemed to have something significant to teach me. I suddenly realized that all of the découpage I'd done back at our old house had been a kind of precognitive experience that had prepared me to make this deeper discovery. These animals were not merely images; they were alive in a completely different way. I was no longer just gluing them to surfaces; I was encountering them as they presented themselves to me in their myriad forms.

A crow stared unyieldingly down at me from a white pine, urging me to return to my desk to write. When I heeded this advice, I felt better. The creatures didn't have to be alive to speak, either. A taxidermied walrus at a shop downtown reminded me that I, like him, am one of a kind. This made me realize that I'd have no competition if I chose a new vocation. And that felt like a truth as well. I relaxed a little more. The Beasties, as I grew fond of calling everything from ladybugs to mythical creatures like dragons and unicorns, were giving me signposts in this unmapped territory I was now traveling.

Despite the incredible opportunity to travel to South Africa, however, I still had to consider travel expenses, four kids, and Mark. Even after getting his approval, I wanted to be absolutely sure it made sense to go. Two days later, sitting next to Suzi as she spoke on her phone to her cousin about the upcoming wedding, I decided to nudge the Universe for a sign and asked the only question I could think of: Where was his bride-to-be's village in relation to Londolozi—a game reserve with several lodges on the border of Kruger National Park. I'd wanted to go there ever since my parents had gushed about their visit years ago. In yet another synchronicity, Martha Beck had also written a bit about her visit there at the end of her book *Steering by Starlight*. If the wedding was nearby, I could build in a visit. But what if it wasn't? Was I still meant to go? We waited quietly while Brian set the phone down to ask Amanda.

When Brian came back to the phone, he told us that Londolozi's owners had built the very school that Amanda had attended as a child—in Hazyview near Kruger Park. Her childhood village was just a few miles down the road from the lodge. A few miles! Suzi and I both started laughing at this massive synchronicity. I had goose bumps buzzing from the top of my head down to my toes, something I'd been experiencing when waking up in the middle of the night all during my sabbatical. I marveled at the laser-like correlation between my African dream and the opportunity I was now being given. Was that how God or the Universe worked?

I had also begun to admit, in secret to myself, that I didn't know how I'd be able to return to medicine. We needed my part-time income, but I wasn't ready to stop exploring. By now, I had a few life-coaching skills, and I decided to set an intention and put it in the hands of the Universe: "If I'm meant to stay on sabbatical and not return to medicine, please show me how." Later that month, Mark was notified that he was getting an unexpected pay hike. The amount of the increase? Almost to the penny the same amount as my part-time salary. I was flabbergasted. Mark raised his eyebrows and shrugged, not wanting to read too much into it. He was pleased and happy for me, but his body language said: "Let's be pragmatic; this money may not last."

Newly aware that my own beliefs might be the only thing holding me back, I began to ask myself the question: "How good are you willing to let it get?"

There are no Hampton Inns out in the South African bushveldt where Suzi and I traveled to negotiate Brian's bride's price. For a few days before the lobola, some local friends snuck us into a vacant cabin at Kruger Park. We were lying in our beds taking a much needed nap when, suddenly, there was a loud knocking on the cabin door. We assumed it was housekeeping, so we asked them to come back later. Then the pounding became angry.

"This is *our* cabin. You need to get out immediately, or we'll call the ranger."

We quickly packed up our suitcases and left, trying to be charming and apologetic as we did so. Suzi's cousin Brian was gone for the day to spend time with Amanda's family, so we were completely alone without a way to contact him or a mode of transportation. Not knowing what else to do, we headed down the dusty Kruger Park road, suitcases rolling behind us, laughing out loud and relieved to be quit of the cabin's testy rightful occupants.

"And you know," I said, "it's weird, but I feel strangely calm right now." Suzi agreed. Even though we'd just been kicked out of our shelter, I didn't feel threatened. In fact, the whole experience felt more like an adventure—almost as if all the work I'd been doing over the last few years had made me spiritually "bulletproof." I *knew* things would be okay. I was simply amazed at how much inner calm I was feeling.

Not five minutes later, one of Brian's friends came down the road toward us. We waved down his car and told him about our eviction. He quickly made a few cell phone calls, and we were whisked into yet another empty cabin that (fingers crossed) was supposed to stay vacant for our last night here. Even better, we decided to call Londolozi and see if they had space for us. I nervously dialed the lodge from a pay phone at the park ranger's station and found there was room at the inn.

After days of coaching from Brian's best friend, a handsome and upbeat Zulu man with a brilliant smile, on how we should proceed during the lobola, we arrived at Amanda's mother's home and were ushered into her spare but comfy living room. We were dressed to the nines, me in a Camaroonian dress I had borrowed from my mom, Brian and his brother Matt in suits, and Suzi in a colorful "lobola" dress a dear friend had sewn for her.

We had brought special gifts—clothing, a blanket, and a particular type of liquor Brian had bought. The gifts were given at designated intervals, and Matt was in charge of "record keeping," taking meticulous notes in a leather-bound journal with a feverish intensity. Our "negotiations" seemed very serious. But Amanda's uncle, who at first seemed humorless, lightened things up after about an hour, and a deal was eventually struck. A little cash and a few small gifts were given in "exchange" for the brilliant and gorgeous Amanda in a symbolic honoring of a long-standing family tradition.

A group of women from the village filled the living room and began dancing and singing with great force and joy, blowing whistles all the while. Then we feasted together, drank a yogurt-based beer out of a gourd, and celebrated the successful agreement. Afterward, we spilled outside to find that the whole courtyard was filled with dancing revelers from the neighborhood. Interconnected, we followed Brian and the women around the packed earth courtyard in a sort of sacred South African bunny hop. The universal language of dance and song made translation completely unnecessary.

Later, we said our goodbyes, and Brian and Amanda drove us down the long dirt road and dropped us off inside Londolozi's gates. We were told to change clothes immediately so that we could join other guests for the evening game safari. We were so moved by our first sight: eight to ten female lions sleeping deeply, post-feast, in a huge somnolent heap, a tail flicking and a nose twitching periodically. In the pride, lady lions do most of the hard work of hunting, and they require deep rest. Suzi and I silently looked at each other with huge eyes, and I mouthed to her: I can't believe this! Suddenly, I realized that, like the lady lions, I'd been working really hard and resting far too little.

During the summer, when I had fallen in love with animal totems, I had shared the Andrews book with Suzi and a group of friends, and we had discussed the idea of animal totems—or Core Beasties, as I'd affectionately dubbed them. I had told her that your own personal animal totem is an animal that has been guiding you and watching over you all your life—probably since childhood. Your totem has the ability to infuse you with power—the peaceful kind of power you need to be effective on your own Hero's journey. It also acts as a kind of "spiritual bouncer" for you, blocking unwanted influences of all kinds. When you listen to your Core Beastie's messages for you, and live your life (metaphorically and sometimes literally) in a way that honors it, your whole life benefits. The spirit of the animal empowers and protects you on your path. So we all decided to reach out to our Beasties.

Suzi realized hers was an eagle, and I shared with her what I'd learned about eagles—that they spend a lot of time conserving energy because they are such effective hunters, and that they need to rest in the nest between hunting flights. "That's *exactly* what I need," said Suzi. "Time to rest in the nest." After that, Suzi changed her work schedule to include more rest time, as eagles do. When she turned down projects that felt draining and took days off just to care for herself, she sometimes laughed and said: "Eagle's gotta rest in the nest."

That weekend, my friends each seemed to discover their own fitting Beastie, or at least a viable candidate to consider. I was so grateful to them for talking about such bizarre topics and embracing these ideas. It made me feel less alone. Yet I was unable to find a special Beastie for myself. You see, there's a hitch; you don't just choose your animal totem; it chooses you.

Here in South Africa, I found myself longing for the kind of personal insight a lifelong bond with an animal spirit can bring. How could I find more calm and peace in my life? I was gaining insights daily by noticing the animals passing in and out of my experience, but which was *the one?* The harder I worked to figure this out, the more elusive the answer seemed. With lions roaring ferociously within earshot, it seemed right to reach out to this other world that was calling me. So I asked for a helpful Beastie to show itself to me in my dreams.

That night, I dreamed of a black mamba, which appeared carved and lifeless on a wooden sign. Mambas are the most feared snakes in South Africa; untreated, their bite is almost always fatal. I woke up startled and sketched out the dream image. To my amazement, the mamba was wrapped around a stick like the rod of Asclepius, a symbol associated with medicine and healing. The Beasties were indeed speaking to me, but I wasn't feeling up to exploring a black mamba. Unlike my earlier journey with the bear, that felt terrifying.

• • •

Clearly, the prescribed and logical ways of navigating the world weren't working for me anymore. I couldn't simply consult a book or a website, or ask a professional. Moreover, I had the sense that I wouldn't be able to carry on without this information. I needed to know—*now*. I knew it was for me to intuit or discover, but I couldn't figure it out in my head. And then I realized that *I needed to use my heart.* After reading Michael Harner's *The Way of the Shaman*, the idea of taking a hallucinogen-induced journey scared the bejesus out of me. But shamanic drumming—that appealed to me.

The particular rhythm of shamanic drumming induces a kind of dream state—a theta-wave state between being awake and asleep, not unlike a REM dream state. This is the state in which some people with autism, and some with inattentive-type ADD, spend more time while awake. Shamans, autistic-spectrum people, and daydreamers are all connected in this way. I figured this kind of journey couldn't be that uncomfortable or risky if I had been unknowingly spending time there already.

Weeks ago, I'd downloaded a drumming recording onto my phone that included guidance from Sandra Ingerman, a shamanic teacher and healer. I hadn't listened to it yet, because I was just a wee bit terrified. I wasn't entirely sure if

I'd have a peaceful experience. And yet, I needed to find a way to go forward. I longed for the clarity and contentment I'd seen others discover.

While talking with our safari ranger in Londolozi, Suzi and I discovered that, for about three hundred dollars, we could request a meeting with a *sangoma*—South Africa's term for a shaman, one who calls the spirits to help others heal and get helpful information. It sounded thrilling to see others practice this ancient art that I'd only read about.

Divination comes in many forms—tea-leaf reading, turtle-shell reading, bibliomancy—but the common denominator in all of these methods is that the interpreter intends to access extraordinary (and otherwise hidden) information to help clients with their quests. Diviners cultivate a sacred relationship with objects and spirits who can reveal these insights.

Suzi and I were both somewhat nervous about what information might be given to us during the session. Our ranger had told us that there were many people in South Africa using shamanic tools as sorcerers rather than healers. On our way to the village to meet with the sangoma, we told Lena, our translator, that we wanted to see how the process worked, but we didn't want to receive a negative prophecy. She smiled and reassured us that they wouldn't tell us anything to hurt us and that she'd be sure to communicate our desires.

We crawled on our hands and knees through a low doorway to enter a round, thatched Shangaan dwelling. Inside, we sat on meticulously woven grass mats in a circle formed by the two women sangomas, Suzi, Lena, and myself. Adopting our host's posture, we got comfortable on the ground with our legs stretched out in front of us,

The sangomas were soft-spoken yet strong women with shining eyes. The apparent leader of the two, a slender woman in her forties with broad smiling cheeks and a small furrow in her brow, greeted us with a nod. Both were dressed in colorful fabric wraps and had white beads in their braided hair. They also wore softly clattering, polished shell anklets and broad fabric straps criss-crossing their chests.

The sangomas spoke with one another in Shangaan and our translator explained that they would begin with Suzi. One of them began to speak and then tossed the "bones"—a small collection of objects—onto the grass mat. Some of these were actual animal bones; others were more like stones. One in particular caught my eye—a small, pitch-black stone. The women conversed back and forth about the pattern and location of the bones as they had landed on the woven mat. Then finally, through the translator, they said to Suzi: "Are you here for a special occasion? It seems one of your ancestors is upset with you."

More discussion ensued, and it was determined that Suzi's deceased paternal grandmother was displeased. Suzi suddenly remembered that she had given a pair of amber earrings that had belonged to that grandmother as a gift to Amanda just a few days ago. When asked, Suzi confirmed that she hadn't asked her grandmother's permission to do this. I immediately flashed back to the lobola ceremony. Amanda had worn the earrings at the beginning of the ceremony, but then, halfway through it, she had reappeared without them. I wondered if she sensed that something was amiss.

The sangomas prescribed a simple ceremony to help Suzi make things right with her grandmother's spirit again. This involved an intention, champagne, some white sugar, and a white towel, all of which we had back in our hotel room. Suzi was instructed to ask her grandmother's forgiveness for not asking her permisson to give the gift.

Now it was my turn, and I asked specifically about a new career: "If I leave medicine to do something else, will it be a good thing?" Saying the words aloud, I recognized that it was an awfully important question to put into the sangomas' hands. I didn't even know them. But Lena, our translator, put me at ease with her warm smile.

The sangomas threw the bones again and

studied the pattern of the fallen objects, speaking quietly with each other in Shangaan. There seemed to be some confusion about the results. One of them pointed to the small, ominous black stone.

After much discussion, they decided to toss the bones again, after which there seemed to be even more confusion and disagreement. Again, the black stone was pointed out. Then they threw the bones a third time. *Seriously?* I threw a questioning look at Suzi and we both shrugged. Perhaps I *did* want to know if there was something bad in the answer. At least then I would be prepared.

After the third toss, the sangoms looked at each other in a resigned way, as if things hadn't gotten any clearer, but they couldn't continue to toss the bones. The translator relayed the outcome: "Your new career choice will be a good thing. Financially and in other ways, you'll be blessed." This gave me relief, because my biggest fears related to money and security. Nothing specific was prescribed or suggested for me, as it had been for Suzi. I was a little disappointed, as I'd also wanted an assignment.

Next, we were instructed to leave the hut and wait outside. Our translator told us the sangomas were going to call their ancestral spirits. As we crawled out of the hut on our hands and knees and looked up, we were astonished to discover that we were not alone. A small crowd of forty to fifty people had gathered outside the hut, forming an informal circle on the dried-mud clearing. Drummers had also appeared. They began to drum—slowly and gently at first, and then more fiercely. Suzi and I sat in wonder on a low wall next to the hut.

As the drumming got louder and faster, we heard powerful singing and shrieking from inside the hut. Then the sangomas came out, one by one, making sounds I had never heard and dancing as I'd never seen. They vibrated, stomped, shimmied, and leapt. They shouted and sang in a mix of tones that ranged from low and guttural to high-pitched, as if different voices were coming through them from another world. A man from the crowd joined them. The noise, the bright sun, the crowd, the drumming—the pure spectacle— was both overwhelming and deeply moving. Emotion welled up from deep within me—joy and gratitude. Tears rolled down my face, drying quickly in the bright sun.

At one point, someone explained to Suzi that the reason they were dancing so hard was to plead with their ancestors' spirits to come out of the trees. And it really felt as if they came. The atmosphere was one of pure power and love. The entire experience felt like an enormous gift to us—these strangers generously allowing themselves to be used in this way for our benefit.

After about twenty minutes, the dancing began to wind down. Before the sangomas returned to the hut to disengage from their ancestral spirits, they came over to us, still in their trances and speaking with the voices of their ancestors. They seemed to be blessing us.

When we returned to our room, Suzi honored her grandmother using sugar packets (she had a sweet tooth) and champagne as gifts offered up on a hotel hand towel. We fell into a deep conversation while standing in the mid-day sun on the deck. Several great memories of her grandmother came flooding back to Suzi, and she said it felt in some ways as if she were saying from another world: "You're not going on this trip without me!"

That night, as I lay in bed replaying the events of the day in my mind, my logical self tried to rationalize the experience. I couldn't be certain about what had *really* happened with regard to spirits. But I knew that we had experienced a beautiful togetherness. The sangomas had listened to us with great intent and were willing to surrender their bodies on our behalf. And the singing, drumming, and dancing had felt overwhelmingly positive, as if the whole village had come out to help us. I knew that I'd experienced healing, and I felt an overwhelming curiosity to learn more about the shamanic path.

CHAPTER 13

Ecstatic Encounters

Only he who attempts the absurd is
capable of achieving the impossible.

Miguel de Unamuno,
Essays and Soliloquies

Mother Bear took me to sit on top of a hill
where we had a view of a vast body of
water, perhaps an ocean. She told me that where
I wanted to go wasn't too far away, and that
all I needed to do was enjoy the journey. Then
we rolled down the hill together like children,
laughing till we cried, dizzy with ecstasy.

Experiences like this helped me through the
utter confusion and fear that gripped me as I
considered a worrying thought: *I can't go back
to medicine.* I wondered, periodically, if maybe
it was all just wishful thinking. Perhaps I wanted
Mother Bear to exist so badly that she seemed
real to me. But each new shamanic experience
showed me that I was not in charge. Every time I
put in my earbuds, listened to the drumming, and

returned to visit the spirit realms, strange things happened—things I couldn't predict. And there seemed to be no way I could be making up these experiences.

When I anxiously asked Mother Bear how to communicate what I was learning most effectively—I was worried about how to build my coaching practice—an enormous tiger suddenly appeared in the already cramped cave to tell me that tigers can communicate with inaudible sounds through mountains and across long distances. I was extremely intimidated and could feel his enormous power. He said: "You can remain hidden and solitary, and there's no need for you to be available for now." Then he took me on a ride. We bounded easily through the woods. He said: "You can make large leaps quickly if you follow this advice."

A few months after returning from South Africa, I sought out a class by a teacher from the Foundation for Shamanic Studies (FSS), which I discovered through Michael Harner's classic work on shamanism, *The Way of the Shaman.* Harner had found ways to synthesize the nearly universal practices of all shamanic cultures so that we Westerners could learn to transform our own lives. I was longing for community but was also respectful of not misappropriating others' traditions. I was drawn to the Foundation because it also seemed to be most concerned with ethics. The last thing I wanted was to be a New Age totem imposter. To my delight, there was an FSS instructor in Minneapolis.

I still wasn't entirely convinced that it was okay to be doing this work (or to be sharing it with others) without careful guidance and blessing from someone steeped in a tradition. Reading dozens of books, however, had helped me recognize that perhaps these shamanic practices were universal. Perhaps you didn't necessarily need to belong to a particular group or be born into a given culture in order to benefit from them. I also had questions. Was there a way to know if what I was experiencing was real? And what more did I need to know?

In a small dance studio in Minneapolis, an FSS class met for a weekend and journeyed over and over, with live drumming, as we lay on yoga mats with our eyes covered. Timothy Cope, our lively and dramatic instructor, presented us with the content in the oral tradition. There were no handouts. He explained the key tenet of shamanism: *Everything that is, is alive.* To do shamanic work, he emphasized, you must have ego—you must know who you are and where you are going—and humility—the humility to recognize that it is not you doing the work. You are merely a conduit.

Timothy also explained that, to do this work,

you must be full of power, and one of the ways to get that power is to dance and sing. His words helped me understand shamanic work more deeply.

"There is very little dogma involved," Timothy explained, "and you must test the truth and validity of everything that I say for yourself. This work is between you and your helping spirits. You alone must experience these things; they cannot be taken on faith."

As the drum beat and people began to dance, I sat on the ground not moving, and I got a nauseous feeling that I suspected was power trying to move through my body as I resisted it. As the first day wore on and people shared their own stories and journeys, I realized that many of the others in the room had been journeying on their own as well. Despite my resistance, I found that more of my questions were answered (and dozens more popped up), and I had a chance to practice using this work to help others who were seeking helpful information or healing. I discovered how joyful it was to journey on behalf of others.

I felt useful in a way I'd never experienced before.

We learned how to perform divination, the art of using stones to seek hidden helpful information to answer questions. I asked a very poignant question: "How can I heal my relationship with my mother?" Things had been strained between us since I went on sabbatical. After asking the stone and studying its many faces, I received this reply: "Through magic and divination." Although this answer may sound vague and completely unhelpful to you, it was so perfect and sweet for me. That day, I let go of trying to "figure out how" to repair what was broken and began to trust that other forces would help us to mend our relationship. Searching for patterns and figures in the stone's intricate face felt strangely easy for me because of the pattern-hunting I had done for two decades with my microscope. It required the same sort of "soft" focus and consideration that helps you discern a pathologic diagnosis.

It was in this setting that I took my first journey to the Upper World to meet a teacher in human form. It wasn't as easy for me as the Lower World journeys had become. It was a more ephemeral and fleeting experience, but I did get a sneak peek at my first spirit teacher, a slender and graceful Hindu deity I immediately recognized as Lakshmi. I could perceive the elegant silhouette of her body. Several months before, I'd been drawn to an Indian painting of a woman sitting on a lotus with two elephants in the background. I impulsively ordered it, even though the style felt totally foreign to me. The oil-on-canvas piece arrived in a tube from India, and I had it framed and hung it in our living room. I later learned that it was a classical depiction of Lakshmi, goddess of spiritual and material prosperity.

When I returned from Minneapolis, I continued to journey nearly daily at home. I holed up in my walk-in closet, the only place in my house where I could journey undisturbed. Each journey and each experience seemed to take me deeper and deeper into ultimately recognizing a new truth: *The spirits are real*—as real as the ones that came and danced in the sangomas' bodies in South Africa. These other realities I was exploring were as real as this earthly one.

Over time, my maps of the spirit worlds and my various spirit helpers became more fleshed out. There were places in each reality where I could return to visit with particular spirits who had certain ways to help me. I learned that the spirit world could be navigated using a multi-dimensional map that I could memorize with my senses. Down and to the left under the huge tree there is a fire. Swim across the water out to the island and head into the jungly area where there's a waterfall. Leap across a river to a spit of land. I began to travel with certain "places" in mind, because I knew a particular spirit would be there to help me with my question or request for healing. This world became very real to me—sort of like my own personal Hundred Acre Wood.

I ordered a drum with a synthetic head and

carefully découpaged its curves with colorful images of wild animals that I reproduced from a turn-of-the-century French children's bingo game I'd been drawn to buy years before. I chose the synthetic drum head because it was more stable than skin drums in humid weather, and I hoped to be able to travel with it. It certainly wasn't like any native drum—or really any drum—I'd ever seen before, and I wondered if I was going about this in the wrong way. But something in me whispered: *Keep going.*

I loved this drum; it felt sacred to me. I taught myself to drum by listening over and over to the recordings I'd collected. I simply replicated the beat and then I practiced the call-back sequences, which signaled to the person on the journey that it was time to return home. Finally, I tried to record myself doing a full fifteen-minute journey and discovered that I could do it.

The more I journeyed, the more healed and whole I felt. I wrote in my journal: "It feels as if my brain is being rewired." The most encouraging thing was that the spirits wanted nothing more than to help me with my ideas and questions. I had somewhere to go with all of my day-to-day confusions. And each time I returned, I felt more at peace.

CHAPTER 14

Doin' the Mamba

You enter the forest at the darkest point,
where there is no path. Where there is a
way or path, it is someone else's path.
You are not on your own path. If you
follow someone else's way, you are not
going to realize your potential.

Joseph Campbell, *The Hero's Journey*

Ever since I'd gotten back from Africa, where I had my first dream of the black mamba, I had become more frustrated with my design work at the office where Suzi and I had been collaborating a few days a week on residential and commercial projects. I've had a love of design ever since my dad built me my first dollhouse, and I often wondered whether it was perhaps a calling. I loved coming up with design concepts and finding unusual and beautiful things to express a client's unique personal aesthetic, but I wasn't as well suited for all the measuring, strategizing, and ordering required to make my concepts a reality.

My friendship with Suzi became strained under the pressure of all the projects we had pending, and I came home exhausted on the days when we worked together. Suzi described my state perfectly: "You're like a sweaty racehorse trapped in the gate. It's as if you just need to run." A part of me wanted to cut to the chase and simply know what I was supposed to become. Whenever I tried to get logical or make sense of it all, I experienced tremendous frustration, as if I were supposed to keep exploring while simultaneously accepting that I couldn't know what it all meant.

Suzi and I had been on parallel journeys of self-discovery ever since we had known each other. And we had shared a lot along the way. As my own clash between work, mothering, and trying to find a purpose deepened, Suzi was experiencing her own life crisis, ultimately turning to twelve-step programs in an attempt to sort out her own stuff. We had constantly traded confidences, spiritual insights, mantras, and frustrations in our joint pursuit of motherhood, marriage, and personal dreams. So it was very difficult for me to consider breaking from her in any way.

I painfully confessed to Suzi that, even after all the work we had done together and all the time she had invested in me during the past year setting up shop, anticipating a long-term collaboration as entrepreneurs, I needed time alone to think and to pursue my new path. I told her that, instead of spending all our time together working, I wanted to get back to focusing on our friendship. Although I tried to soften the blow, I could tell from her voice that my news was surprising and hurtful. Even so, like the true friend she is, she immediately said: "I understand."

During this liminal period, fear periodically crept up on me. If someone asked what I was doing with my time now that I wasn't at the hospital anymore or working with Suzi, I went into a tailspin. And, of course, I worried about money. I'd historically been our financial planner and money manager. Sometimes, I felt as if I was the only one who knew what was going on with our finances. When I got our post-Africa credit-card bill (roughly two months' income), I showed it to Mark, feeling guilty about the money I'd spent. But how could I not have gone? And if I was partly responsible for getting us into this financial pickle, wasn't it my responsibility to figure a way out of it?

Mark just shrugged and said we'd just have to look more carefully at what we were doing. I admitted that going back to work at the hospital two days a week would solve a lot of problems, but just thinking about doing that made me feel as if I were shrinking inside. Mark interrupted my grim musing.

"But you seem so happy. Why would you go back now? Why don't you just keep going on this path?"

His comment was so kind. The moment he said it, I felt so supported. I could sense that, at least for the time being, he wasn't worried about our finances. More important, he had faith in me. I was ready for a little of that.

With Mark's blessing, I called my section chair at the hospital to say that I wanted to extend my radical sabbatical for three more months—to a whopping total of six months. Three months had sounded like a lifetime when it began, but now it felt like the blink of an eye. I told him I needed a bit more time. To my surprise, he cheerfully agreed and said that extending the sabbatical wouldn't be a big problem.

Eventually, at the end of my six-month sabbatical, I struck a deal with my fellow partners. Instead of returning to work regularly, I was retained as a partner and given "casual status," meaning that, if I was desperately needed, they could call me in to cover for a day now and then. And I kept my hospital privileges.

As my journeying continued, I felt stronger. I decided it was time to face the black mamba that had appeared in my dreams in South Africa. I had learned from my reading that Beasties that scare you often carry a particularly important message.

I watched a lot of BBC footage of black mambas. I took note of their elegance—especially as they swam through water or lifted their head and body into the air—their beauty, and their deadly venom. Sometimes, studying the things that scare the bejesus out of me helps me relax.

I used a technique of shamanic journeying I had learned from the book *Conscious Dreaming* by Robert Moss to re-enter my dream with the mamba. I set an intention to re-enter the dream to see how it finished. As I walked down my gravelly tunnel and stepped out into the Lower World, Mother Bear walked me right back into the dream and stayed by my side. Mamba appeared immediately, just as I'd requested, only now she was no longer lifeless on a carved wooden sign, but slithering through the grass. Mother Bear and I followed her, and I asked her: "How are you here to help me?"

Mamba gave me no reply but slithered quickly forward. I followed her, and, as I did, I became a snake as well. Suddenly she stopped, reared up, and began to dance, swaying her head back and forth in the air. It seemed as if she wanted me to mirror her moves, to dance with her. I tried to urge her forward, but her image blurred, and she seemed to become more aggressive, truly frightening. I refused to dance with her and indicated silently that I'd rather keep moving. "Can't we go wherever we were headed before?" I pleaded.

Mamba threatened to bite me if I refused to dance with her. *It's to help you get healing,* she made me understand. She was confident, elegant, and unpredictable—and she wasn't going to back down.

I stood my ground, refusing. Then she struck fast and bit me in my right shoulder near the neck. I was momentarily terrified. I knew it was a journey, but it felt so *real*. I reached out for Mother Bear, who seemed completely unconcerned, as if to say: "Go on and take your whoopin' so we can go home."

When I returned from the Lower World, I was lying in the dark on the floor of my walk-in closet. Suddenly, I thought I heard something rustling in the corner and actually feared for a second that it was a black mamba. Then I realized there was nothing there. I was safe. I was home. I also knew I wasn't done with Mamba yet.

Why didn't I step up to dance? Maybe next time I would have to be clearer about my intention so that weird stuff wouldn't happen. I'd hoped Mamba would just tell me something juicy. I was embarrassed to dance with her and didn't understand the purpose of it. Why did I have to *do* anything? Was it all a metaphor? How many times in my life had I been asked to step up but refused or been so terrified that I tried to avoid it in any way that I could? I refused to ride horses but ended up loving it. I refused to emcee one of my *a capella* group's concerts because I feared I wouldn't be able to duplicate a previous triumph. I refused to go into direct patient care, choosing pathology instead, so I wouldn't have to face emotional entanglements with dying patients. There were so many times when I had rebelled, balked, or stood on the sidelines rather than stepping up. Now I was sick and tired of not standing up to my fears. So, a few weeks later, I gathered all my courage and lay back down on my closet floor to visit the black mamba yet again.

This time, it was different. I was scared, mind you, but I surrendered. I took Mother Bear along, of course. We re-entered the dream, and I told Mamba I was ready to dance. She nodded and gestured to us to follow her out into an open field—breathtakingly beautiful, wild, and open, like the plains of Mongolia. Once there, she indicated that it was time to dance. Bear and I danced back and forth, trying to imitate Mamba's movements. At first, it was awkward trying to dance like a snake. It's not easy to mamba. As we danced, my logical mind was full of questions. What was the point of all this? And then, *I had a wordless experience.* I became filled with a peaceful, powerful energy that caused me to grow and grow and grow in size, until I towered over Mamba and Mother Bear, like a Macy's Thanksgiving Day parade balloon.

I wasn't sure what had just happened, but when I returned to my closet floor, I knew I'd experienced honest-to-goodness power. It turns out that power feels like a peaceful knowing— like being utterly supported and loved by the Universe. It felt totally fantastic. It seemed that, although the process of owning my power was terrifying, power itself was not. I just needed to be *willing* to dance. Like a fearless motherfucker.

Becoming a life coach with ADD sounded so sexy on paper. I'd thought that establishing and running my coaching practice would feel like being Richard Branson, the founder and leader of Virgin airlines (who was also diagnosed with ADD). I thought I'd simply take his advice to "Screw it. Let's do it" and take off flying. In reality, it was hard.

It was a dream come true to "be the boss of me," to be free to be creative all the time in any way I desired. Yet I was longing for the structure the hospital practice had given me. Instead of having my schedule dictated, I now had to create my own. I also needed to go out in the world to invite others to try my services. Worst of all, I'd been told I needed to create some "business systems."

With only a Facebook page and a YouTube channel as my platform, I had my work cut out for me. I was working from home and had four kids who needed snacks packed for school, help with math, and shuttling to a full slate of activities. I frequently thought to myself: *What have I done?*

At the suggestion of my psychologist and physician, I'd been on a trial of a long-acting stimulant for my ADD ever since my summer sabbatical. I'd heard how much stimulant medication could help with the feeling of being overwhelmed that is associated with ADD. Thanks to the drug, I could now focus on accounting for hours without thinking once about peonies, elephants, or Tina Fey. In fact, it allowed me to be *so* hyper-focused for *so* many hours on end that I worked myself into deep exhaustion. It worried me and it didn't escape Mark either. I played around with short- versus long-acting versions of the drug. Some nights, it was hard to get the deep rest I needed. Taking a nap was out of the question; my mind wouldn't shut down. I felt productive, but also as if I had a six-hour executive-function hard-on. It was a little too much of a good thing.

One evening, George did one of the strangest things I'd ever seen him do. After dinner, without our knowing, he slipped away into my closet and donned every single piece of my favorite clothing—giant party-sized sunglasses, multiple scarves and necklaces, Ugg boots, a floppy summer beach hat, and, to top it all off, a coyote-fur vest bought long before I knew about the sacredness of Beasties. Then he half stumbled and half walked, as if in a trance, into the living room.

We all sat in stunned silence, dying to know what would happen next. He moved like a zombie with vertigo toward the couch and said, in a loud high-pitched monotone: "I am Sarah Seidelmann, and I am *sooo* tired." Then, in a final act of dramatic glory, he did a face-plant with a thud onto the couch. His performance complete, we all collapsed into laughter.

No wonder he was worried about me! Trying so hard to get where I'm going had me completely shattered.

Years later, I returned from grocery shopping one day to find George in the living room, sitting on the floor surrounded by seven or eight burning votive candles. I was temporarily stunned. I stared, trying not to look shocked.

"What's up?" I ventured gently.

"I'm just trying to figure things out right now," George said. He was sitting in a relaxed lotus position (holy smokes!), a posture in which I had never witnessed him before. That morning he'd learned that he hadn't made the hockey team. It was heartbreaking to see him so disappointed. But it was quietly thrilling to observe him going through his own process of resolution. It wasn't that he was overtly accepting my search for answers in practices like shamanism and healing. He was just showing me that he, also, had a spiritual side.

Several months later, with guidance from my spirits, I quit taking stimulants. My softness returned, and I found a natural rhythm of deep rest and work. Visiting Mother Bear frequently helped a lot. For me, going pharmaceutical-free was the best decision. It was still much harder to do things like pay bills and work on some aspects of my writing without medication, but it no longer felt as if I were living on borrowed time by working so intensely.

Despite the immense challenges, things slowly began to come together. I got a website up and began sending out regular newsletters and doing some rudimentary accounting. The podcast on animal totems that I co-created with a colleague seemed to be taking off, with hundreds of downloads each week. And somehow, I'd been crowned (albeit by a small group) the "Animal Totem Queen," known for helping people learn how to receive the messages Beasties were trying to deliver. I comforted myself with the thought that I still had a legitimate job to return to if my dreams failed to materialize. Luckily, help was on the way.

CHAPTER 15

Alice Arrives

"Who is Alice?" asked Mother.
"Alice is somebody that nobody
can see," said Frances.

Russell Hoban, *A Birthday for Frances*

I continued to journey frequently—at least a few times a week and sometimes more. A new spirit helper came forth—an Asian elephant named Alice. I learned it is poor form in some cultures to discuss your spirit helpers openly, but Alice informed me that she enjoys the limelight and wants me to share our connection.

Alice made herself known slowly, perhaps so I could get used to the idea of her. Looking back, she had actually appeared long before Mother Bear, though I had not been conscious of who she was. Years before I even understood who spirits like Alice were, she'd emerged as an image in a collection of vintage chromolithographs of wild animals gathered during my all-consuming découpage phase. I had color photocopied a natural history illustration from the 1800s and cut out an elephant from its background. I remember noticing the kind look she had in her eyes. She seemed to me to be a very warm, pleasing pachyderm, beautifully soft gray, with just the right number of wrinkles. She grew more real in my consciousness, in the way a Polaroid oozes into existence. But when we first met, I wasn't ready to receive a spirit visitor, so Alice took her time.

As I began taking more shamanic journeys to the Upper World, elephants appeared in large herds, even though that realm was supposedly filled with spirits in human form. I had to remind myself that, in these realities, there are no limits. One day, a single elephant appeared. She was standing on a spit of land formed where two rivers met. I wondered if this was the same elephant I'd become aware of through my paper cut-outs and découpage. I asked her and she confirmed that she was. Over time, as I visited her again and again, Alice told me her name.

I record my conversations with Alice in a journal, along with the outcomes of applying the insights I receive from her. Alice's wisdom has helped me tremendously. Often, she laughs about my worldly concerns—not in a cruel way, but in a kind, light-hearted, head-shaking elephant way, as if to say that I shouldn't take my fears so seriously. When I fret and ask frustrated questions—What's going to happen next? Where will I end up? What will it look like?—Alice responds cheerfully that there will be a lot of elephants cheering me on and that I should look for them. Immediately after hearing this, my Facebook wall began filling with postings of elephants from friends and followers.

When I wonder how I can feel entirely harmonious with Mark, Alice responds: Don't worry about him today; just get your own feel-good on and have fun! When I take this advice, I end up having a great day and things with Mark *are* strangely easy. When I tell Alice that I'm worried that I don't know how I can serve the highest good, she answers: Be yourself! Everybody else is taken. Have fun!

These experiences with Alice often show me how much I belong. When she took me to swim with the whole elephant family, I experienced an unbearable lightness of being, a joyous letting-go filled with childlike wonder. Their enormous, heavy bodies were rendered light and buoyant by the water. They staged a grand underwater ballet, their tree-trunk limbs churning effortlessly beneath the surface as they glided gracefully about. Sprays of water from trunks used as playful water cannons added refreshment. Periodically, they collided ever so gently with one another, just for fun.

Swimming alongside these magnificent beings in this expansive, effervescent rumpus, I began to feel so much love and connection that I thought I would burst. Tears ran down my cheeks and into my ears. Here, with this profoundly sweet family, I understood that I was a part of their circle. Perhaps Alice appeared and escorted me to swim with the elephants because she knew I was better off buoyant. I never wanted to forget this feeling of tender comingling, and I hoped to emulate it back in the ordinary world.

Alice is sometimes zany and theatrical. But she can also be quiet and sensitive. I've heard that spirits often appear to us in ways that we will find appealing. I had a default tendency to get too serious, to squelch the Steve Martin part of my brain—my Heyoka self. Heyoka is the sacred clown contrarian of the Lakota people of the Great Plains of North America who knows how to restore balance by creating mayhem, violating taboos, and acting out or saying things considered unthinkable by society.

To be clear, Alice isn't an archetype or an alter ego. I couldn't be in a companionable relationship with a concept. Archetypes don't converse, surprise, swim, do healing work, or spontaneously dance at the drop of a hat. For me, Alice is as real and distinctive as any other being in my life—except for the fact that she doesn't manifest on the earth. She wears beautiful chains of peonies around her neck that I can press my face into for comfort and to *know* she is truly here with me. Spending time in these realms with Alice is a curious experience of knowing without knowing—of knowing through body/heart/mind/spirit.

You may argue that Alice is merely an aspect of me, and I'd have to agree. She is a manifestation of God and the Universe. And so am I. In a way, I am Alice and Alice is me, in the same way that you are me and I am you. And yet Alice is also separate from me, in the way that you and I are distinct yet connected by spirit.

Though she is a spirit, Alice can also be pragmatic. When I am confused about how to work productively, she gives me helpful sample schedules—work in early morning, then walk the dog, not the other way around. She also gives me metaphors to help me complete particular projects. Step carefully from lily pad to lily pad. Don't hurry or you'll fall into the river! When I was concerned about using salty language in my second book, she gave me this clarifying advice: Stay out of muddy quagmires. It's the spirit in which things are said that matters.

And there's another thing I want to make clear: Alice is a dear spirit companion, but she doesn't want to control my destiny. In contrast, she cheers me on in whatever destiny I choose. When I ask her what I should create, she always reminds me that it is up to me. For me, Alice is a source of clarity and wisdom about the truth of all matters.

While some of the things she tells me may seem obvious, they aren't to me at the time. I ask Alice the questions I most desperately need answered so I can keep going. *Alice encourages me.*

Alice knows when I can handle her cajoling and when I can't. On days when I am despairing, she gathers the whole herd around me and I feel embraced and loved on a level I've never known. When I feel terribly alone or more helpless than usual, she holds me in an embrace so sweet and peaceful that *I know,* no matter what, I'll be okay.

One day, while traveling and experiencing an achy loneliness, I awoke in my hotel room, stared at the ceiling, and noted that the sprinkler system resembled the head of an elephant. I knew in a split second that Alice was right there with me. It sounds strange and implausible, I know—a sprinkler-head darshan or divine vision? Perhaps it sounds like a hallucination or merely wishful thinking. All I can report is that it brought me a deep sense of comfort, of knowing I was loved and not alone.

At other times, Alice has appeared to me in Nature—in a piece of wood near a streambed where I am meditating, or in a stone. She shows up in unexpected places, a sweet and powerful presence that I know I can call on anytime.

Charlie and Josephine asked about Alice when they saw images of her on my computer screen and on my mouse pad. I explained: "This is

Alice. She's a spirit elephant who helps me—kind of like you having stuffed animals you can talk to who comfort you, or an invisible friend. That's Alice."

Charlie immediately understood and smiled. Josephine seemed to comprehend, if not entirely approve. Katherine overheard and smiled but said: "Okay, Mom. But you probably shouldn't say that kind of stuff to other people." When I left to travel, Charlie asked: "Will Alice be going with you?" I replied that of course she would. He smiled and hugged Mr. Pillow-pet, his own green fluffy spirit friend, to his heart.

CHAPTER 16

Hugging Horses

Things that matter
don't necessarily make sense.

Russel Hoban, *Turtle Diary*

Working all the time, reinventing ourselves, and raising kids had taken its toll. Mark and I decided we were long overdue for a getaway, and we headed to St. George, Utah. During the flight, I experienced the complete opposite of enlightenment. Everything my beloved did drove me bat-shit crazy.

We'd both been reading tons of books on self-help. Mark had been studying in Tom Brown Jr.'s Tracker School for several years. Our self-awareness had been growing. I now understood that Mark was a mirror for my consciousness, but right at that moment I couldn't have cared less. The biggest problem? He didn't seem to mind my crankiness at all. Apparently, his mindfulness had overtaken mine. Dammit. To add to the affront, at the spa where we were staying, he was super-effusive with the water-aerobics ladies. This made him even more difficult to bear. Now, he was mindful *and* popular.

I was drawn to signing up for the Mustang Experience, an opportunity to interact with and learn from wild horses. During coach training, I had heard of Equus therapy and was intrigued. Mark wasn't interested in joining me, quietly remarking that he didn't need to spend money on extra activities, because he was *already* at a spa. My money guilt aside, however, I felt excited about this opportunity. I was curious to find out what a (formerly wild) horse could teach me.

The spa's driver dropped me off on a desert road at a small collection of trailers and told me he'd be back to get me in a few hours. Three women sporting flannel, well-worn denim, and cowboy boots came out to greet me. My handlers watched me carefully, as if I were a new horse and they didn't quite know what to think of me.

The mustang ladies took me to a round pen containing several horses. The horses ran around and frolicked while one lady pointed out the leader. "You see that one there? She's in charge. They all look to her to see what they should be doing—to stay safe. That other one there being goofy and kicking up his heels? He's the clown."

It was fascinating—a tiny horse society.

"Horses are matriarchal," the mustang lady told me. "So, if you want to lead a horse, you need to show them you're worthy of trust. You've got to convince them they should keep an eye on you if they want to stay out of danger. You've gotta be steady and calm."

I was invited to enter the pen and told to stand in its center. "See if you can get the horse to follow you," they said, "to do what you ask. It's all about your energy. You can raise your arms up and ask them with your energy to speed up. Then you can try bringing your arms down and ask them to slow down."

Apparently, mustangs can smell a rat if you are scared, hesitant, or hepped up on your own bullshit. I must have been in a peaceful state, however, because, when I raised my arms as instructed and envisioned the horse running, he did. When I lowered my arms and slowed my energy, he slowed. We were in sync. We did a few more variations on this theme, but, in general, the horse was apparently accepting my leadership.

It seemed so easy that I began to suspect this was only happening because of some training the horse had. Nevertheless, my instructor smiled; she seemed surprised and pleased with my success. Apparently, this cleared me for the next level. Exercise one: Success!

Note to reader: Be wary of early success in the spiritual field!

Soon it was time for the big-finish mustang exercise—the horse hug. One of the mustang ladies asked me, in her brawny but lilting voice, if I was ready. Feeling breezy and confident from my earlier success, I assured her that I was. I was a lead mare on fire.

"This part of the experience is *really* powerful," the woman told me. "It's brought many tough cases—hardcore addicts, depressed teenagers, and others—to tears. It's truly capable of causing deep transformation and enormous emotional shifts."

Suddenly, I was caught off guard. Maybe I should just stick with my earlier success. I wasn't so sure I could also be a successful horse hugger. I mean, I liked hugging, but embracing an equine seemed very—well, different. I sensed an expansive and growing canyon between the woman's excitement and my own desire to move forward with a life-altering horse embrace. We walked over to another fenced-in area in which a horse with painted coloring was tied up to the rail. He eyed me reluctantly. We approached the tied-up horse and my instructor demonstrated the way to wrap my arms around the horse's neck and then twist, so that my body swung gently in front of him, allowing our hearts to connect more directly—horse heart to human heart.

We ran through the horse-hug procedure in much the same way I've heard that Olympians mentally run through their events, envisioning a gold medal before actually securing it. When I laid my hands lightly on the horse's neck, he leaped forward slightly, as if rejecting me (his rope allowed him only a few inches of leeway). "Whoa there," my instructor gently scolded him, then turned to me. "Do you understand what you need to do?" she asked, her eyes searching my face.

I nodded. It was now or never. I was about to launch into the hug when she abruptly cut in. "Hold up, Sarah. Not yet. Just give us a minute." While I held off, I regarded the horse. It seemed to me that he was nothing but a pawn. What choice did he have? He was a hugging-horse-for-hire, and I was just another hug-hungry customer from the spa.

The three ladies ran off to a lean-to for some lawn chairs. They lined them up shotgun style about twelve feet from me and settled down in their seats, then grabbed their insulated coffee containers and commenced sipping, readying for my Big Show. One of them bellowed: "Okay, Sarah. Go ahead!" I must have look dazed, because she had to holler again: "You can hug him now!"

In that moment, everything seemed so wrong. I longed to pull a big curtain between me and my horse friend, and the overeager cowgirl audience. I wanted a little privacy for myself and for him. My transcendent experiences weren't for public viewing. I was trying to have a sacred horse hug, even if he was tied up and likely serving me against his will.

I longed for the cosmic shift, *the awakening by equine embrace*. I glanced hastily at our attentive audience of ranchy women and wanted to run. Or maybe I was telepathic and it was the horse. Leaning over in the least offensive way I could, I wrapped my arms lightly around the horse's neck. Then, in a hesitant, slow, and extremely sketchy sort of surrender, I allowed myself to swing, ever so gently, down in front of his enormous chest. As I dangled myself in front of him, I felt him brace for impact, his whole body tensing in deep-seated disapprobation.

The horse was reticent but committed. I imagined a speech bubble above his head: If I just get through one more of these hugs, I can go for a smoke. Then just one more hug after lunch, and I can send some money home to Grandma and the foals back in Green Valley. I'll suffer through this so that one day we can all be free again!

Great—my horse was freaking Nelson Mandela reincarnated.

As I rode back in the spa's van on the dusty road, I replayed the embrace, searching for some great revelation. I couldn't sense any significant emotional shift. It was just really, *really* awkward. I'd had an epic horse-intimacy failure and I felt confused. It felt impossible for me to discover anything deeper. What did it all *mean?* At dinner, Mark told me about the great time he'd had doing yoga and water aerobics. "And it didn't cost anything extra," he added.

Later that week, as we stayed our last night in Las Vegas before flying home, something in me finally softened. We had a wacky good time eating sushi and drinking beer while we watched pirates do acrobatics and shoot at each other from the masts of a sailing ship. We wound down the night at the top of the (fake) Eiffel tower eating fancy cheeses, holding hands, and toasting ourselves while staring out into the rainbow-colored skyline below.

CHAPTER 17

The Healing Stones

In many shamanic societies, if you
came to a shaman or medicine person
complaining of being disheartened,
dispirited, or depressed, they would ask
one of four questions. When did you stop
dancing? When did you stop singing?
When did you stop being enchanted
by stories? When did you stop finding
comfort in the sweet territory of silence?

Angeles Arrien, *The Four-Fold Way*

Mark and I decided to attend a shamanic workshop in the desert near Joshua Tree National Park in southern California. This particular school worked with the teachings and tools of shamans from the Andes and attracted a fun-loving and fantastic group of people from all across the country. There were start-up CEOs, advertising gurus, copywriters, nutritionists, nurses, physicians, chiropractors, and creative entrepreneurs. Everyone seemed pretty normal (and by that, I mean gainfully employed), which was deeply comforting. By now, I was beginning to wonder if anyone who held down an actual paying job did this kind of spiritual work.

When we pulled into the parking area, we saw a dilapidated sign that read "Institute of Mental Physics." Yes, that sounded about right. The work of personal transformation I'd been doing lately felt really hard, like mental physics. Or maybe spiritual gymnastics. We argued about the best place to park. We were both nervous, and I was feeling more like Crusty the Clown from *The Simpsons* than a spiritual being.

During one exercise, we were told that the stones we'd been asked to bring from home would become tools for our own healing. "So just hold your stones close and really connect with them," our instructor said. "Dance with them; bring this connection you share to life! These are your healing stones—for your healing work." Another instructor cranked up the tunes—a funky, Bohemian riff with a heavy drumbeat— and our group of about fifty adults all began to shuffle around the floor, cradling our stones like newborn babies.

On some level, I knew this was sacred work, but there was another part of me (the *South Park* part) that wouldn't have it. So, as I was sashaying around the deeply padded floor clutching my stones—a piece of lapis, a chunk of black volcanic basalt, and an old, fossilized deer hip bone I'd recovered from the riverbed near our house—I was thinking to myself: We look ridiculous! It was just too New Age. This was *way* too far a bridge for us to cross.

Then (oh no!), I caught the eye of a fellow student who was a bit of a sacred clown herself. We both started laughing at our stone-hugging boogie, which had now shifted into a slow jam. I was suddenly back at the seventh-grade dance in the cafeteria with Lionel Richie's *Penny Lover* playing, only I was fondling my odd bevy of rocks instead of a scrawny prepubescent male.

Over a dinner of quinoa and gluten-free everything, my fellow clown and I busted a gut replaying the awesome silliness of our stone-grooving. "I was really having a hard time getting into it and then I caught your eyes and it was *over*. I couldn't stop laughing," I confessed. She agreed. Despite my resistance, however, I had to acknowledge that I really enjoyed the material they were teaching. "I'm absolutely loving the beauty of all the stones people have brought and the way the instructors dramatically spit and spray the *agua de florida* all over people when they are doing the healing work! It's crazy awesome! I want more! Will somebody *please pass the shaman sauce?!*" We all burst into laughter. Shaman sauce was truly what we were all seeking—some sort of magical balm in a bottle to restore our souls.

But a part of me wanted to question my laughter. Maybe I wasn't taking the sacred seriously enough, or maybe the sacred needed to be serious, or maybe I was simply immature and needed to learn to become more still. Later, when I asked another student about our dances-with-stones laughter, she said: "I have two words for you—Dalai Lama. The guy is constantly cracking jokes and laughing his head off, and he's one of the holiest humans on the planet!" So maybe that part of my brain *was* the divine part.

The weekend we spent at the school featured an introduction to the culturally based shamanism of the Incan people, which was quite different from the core shamanism I'd been studying. A shaman from Peru was on site to do initiations for us. I was fascinated by the beauty of these ancient practices and the ritual tools from the Andes—the stones and the colorful woven mesa cloths that held so much meaning.

What didn't feel quite as right for me was the prescribed nature in which all the teachings were done. There was definitely more rigidity, more dogma. To open the four directions, you called in prescribed spirits rather than discovering your own. In that way, it felt a little more like a religion to me. You went off on journeys with descriptions of the characters you'd meet and where you'd go in the spirit realities. I preferred a more open-ended style of teaching, where students weren't given any specific answers or directed to call in any particular spirits. They were sent off to the spirit worlds to discover everything on their own. Perhaps because I wasn't born into this lineage, experiential methods felt more authentic to me.

Little did I know how powerfully this experience with the healing stones would affect my life.

I returned home with my stones, curious and eager to try working with them on my own. I even invited each of my kids to have a "healing session" with me. The two younger ones volunteered immediately. It seemed that Josephine, now eight, had a stomachache.

We went into the small extra bedroom I had claimed as my "healing room." It had a low antique Chinese dresser *cum* altar lacquered in ocean blue with golden flourishes whose many little drawers held my journals and other special trinkets. There was also an incense burner in the shape of a dragon, a candle, and a few other meaningful symbols—a framed photo of one of our garden peonies blossoming to represent abundance, a shiny glazed black bear that Katherine had made, and an elaborately painted Indian elephant. Hanging on the wall above it was the large portrait of Lakshmi depicting purpose or *dharma*, a complicated Sanskrit concept that, for me, means that, when we use our gifts, our work will sweeten the world.

I lit a candle, opened sacred space, and encouraged Josephine to begin by making a collage to show me how her tummy felt. She shrugged and examined the shallow bowl filled with a collection of sticks, leaves, seeds, stones, and dried flower petals. Then she slowly created a collage that, at first, appeared to be a tangled jumble.

"Okay," I said. "Now choose one of my stones and gather up all the pain in your tummy and all of the feeling around it and blow it into the stone three times, taking your time between breaths."

When she finished, she lay down, and I got out my pendulum to help me determine in which direction the chakra, or energy center, was spinning and how fast. I was no expert, but I had built up enough experience with the pendulum that I felt I could work with it. Assessing chakras seemed very different in some ways from pathologic diagnosis, because chakras are not visible like the cells on a Pap smear, for example. You have to sort of surrender and to feel and trust what you are sensing. Yet, as I practiced, I was able to perceive differences that surprised me. I swung the pendulum over her belly, moving up the chakras, until it indicated where the energy was blocked by spinning counterclockwise. I placed the stone in that area.

"Now I want you to take some deep breaths and, as you blow out, continue to send all of that pain, that yucky feeling in your tummy, right into the stone. The stone can handle it, okay?"

Josephine nodded. She began to breathe in and blow out, over and over. After a few minutes had passed, I sensed that there had been some sort of release in her body as she let out a sigh. So I rechecked the blocked area with my pendulum. Now the energy seemed to be flowing freely and I sensed that the affected chakra seemed to be spinning smoothly again. I then illuminated all of Josephine's chakras, filling them with light and empowering them from the heavens. As I did, I could feel a sweetness, a peace, enveloping us.

Suddenly, I felt as if it didn't matter what I did with these tools in the future. *This moment was enough.* I'd been given a gift that allowed me to connect sweetly with my daughter on a deeper level. When the healing was complete, I noticed that Josephine was visibly softer. "My tummy feels better," she told me.

I invited her to look at her tummy collage again. "If it feels the same, you can leave it as is. Or if it feels different, you can make any changes you want to show what's different." She immediately began to rearrange things with an air of quiet excitement. What she ended up with looked much more orderly and symmetric. Had some kind of order been restored?

"Can you see it?" she asked.

I cocked my head. "I'm not sure. I see that it's much different than before."

Josephine grinned. "It's an *angel.*"

Suddenly, I recognized the angel's agate head and feathery grass wings. This surprised and touched me so much. Something about doing this work with Josephine, an open and nonjudgmental child, helped me to see its pure power and profound beauty in a whole new light.

CHAPTER 18

Family Healing

In the shamanic view, mental illness
signals "the birth of a healer," explains
Malidoma Patrice Somé. Thus, mental
disorders are spiritual emergencies,
spiritual crises, and need to be regarded
as such to aid the healer in being born.

Stephanie Marohn, *Waking Times*

My younger sister, Maria, now in her early
forties, had led a difficult life, struggling
mightily with depression and anxiety since
early adolescence. Shortly after she was released
from an inpatient psychiatric treatment center,
I flew out to L. A. to visit her. We spent a great
morning together with her good friends, Amy and
Katie. But afterward, she became unexpectedly
tearful as I sat alone with her in her living
room. "I just don't feel safe here," she said.
"I'm feeling really bad. I'm so sorry." Later
that day, she called to say that she wouldn't be
coming back to her house to sleep, describing
how she had acted out in her day treatment that

morning in a way that ensured she would be readmitted.

I told her that she needed to trust that instinct. "Only you can know just what you need," I said, completely caught off guard. I'd thought things were better. I wanted to wish all of Maria's discomfort and fear away. I wanted my presence to be enough. Of course it wasn't. Selfishly, I'd longed to spend a week building a reserve of happy memories together. It had been a long time, and I was afraid that we were still caught in our old established roles—I as rescuing older sister and she as troubled victim. I needed to take a step back and realize that this problem wasn't mine to fix. I could be loving and supportive, but it was up to Maria to determine what she needed to feel better. All I could offer was my presence.

As I considered this, I was reminded of the mythical insight into mental illness expressed by Joseph Campbell in *Schizophrenia: The Inward Journey*.

> A [mental health] breakdown is an inward and backward journey to recover something missed or lost, and to restore, thereby, a vital balance. So let the voyager go. He has tipped over and is sinking, perhaps drowning. Don't cut him off from it; help him through.

This shamanic or mythical view of mental-health crises as initiations—as a way for a person to receive a gift—was so inspiring to me. I wanted to draw on it to help Maria heal. How could I use it to help her through? Then I had a thought. I knew Maria didn't believe in God and the Beastie spirits and all that stuff, but I wondered if she would consider having a shamanic healing. I told her that I'd seen it really help and that, in fact, it had helped me. I offered to contact a local healer.

"Sure, I'll try anything," Maria responded. The shamanic healer recommended by friends wasn't available but passed along a warning: "Hospitals can be funny about shamanic work, so it can be tricky. But tell Maria that, once she's out, I'll be happy to work with her." My heart sank. Deep down, I sensed that, if Maria's spirit wasn't healed, all the medications in the world weren't going to give her lasting peace of mind. I asked the healer if she'd walk me through what I could do to help Maria. I wrote it all down and double-checked everything. I didn't want to mess this up.

When I visited Maria, I found her sitting in the common area of the ward, chatting with a small group of visiting friends. She looked frail but luminous. Several disheveled and very dispirited-looking patients in hospital-issue pajamas shuffled around us as we talked. Just seeing the other patients looking so despondent made me afraid for her. This felt to me like the last place a person could get well.

Maria and I visited for a while and then I decided to make my offer. I told her that the healer I had contacted wasn't able to see her until after she was released, but that I was willing to try to do a healing for her right now. She agreed. After checking with a rather gruff-spoken nurse, who told us to leave the door open and gave us no more than five minutes, we went into Maria's room, and I had her lie on the bed. I felt slightly nervous, rushed and exposed, but I was determined to try anyway. I wanted so badly to help. At the same time, I knew that it was up to Maria to be open to healing, and the fact that she was encouraged me.

I opened sacred space in a simple fluid motion and then began the process of working with the energy centers or chakras in her body as I had been instructed over the phone. It was a procedure specifically for people who were in a state of great imbalance. It was all so new to me, and I had so little experience, that a part of me felt as if I were just going through the motions. As I worked slowly from the base of her torso upward to the crown of her head, Maria's body shuddered out three or four sobs, which surprised me and caught me off guard. Something seemed to be moving—or perhaps was being released. I also realized that this was the first authentic emotion I had sensed from her other than fear since I'd arrived in L. A. I finished up and closed the sacred space, grateful for the exchange we had just had.

"It's done," I told her softly.

She responded with tears in her eyes that spilled over down her cheeks. "Thank you for doing that."

"Thank you for letting me do it."

In the weeks that followed, Maria made a slow and steady recovery with the help of her physician, friends, and community. I was grateful to have been part of that support.

It wasn't just my immediate family who experienced degrees of despair on a regular basis. My dad's mother, Lee, had been a psychiatric nurse (married to my grandfather, a psychiatrist) who became a chronic alcoholic. She died tragically in a house fire that started while she was smoking and drinking in bed. They discovered her body the next day when her neighbor found that the wall they shared was warm to the touch. I never realized it before, but the way that she died was not only tragic; it was also potentially significant.

I'd learned during my first formal training in shamanism about the difference between the loving and compassionate spirits of the Upper and Lower worlds, and Middle World spirits. The spirits of the Middle World—the nonordinary aspect of where we live on earth—are a mixed bag. Some are suffering beings. For example, the spirits of those who die suddenly and unexpectedly—in a car accident, a fire, or even in a suicide—may not have yet realized that they are no longer alive, so they are sometimes confused and suffering, searching for loved ones. Without a body, of course, these spirits are no longer able to communicate in the usual way, and sometimes attach themselves to others, attempting to express themselves through their lives and physical bodies, or to influence them. That's essentially what "spiritual intrusion" is.

I wondered if Grandmother Lee could be one of those confused, stuck spirits. Could that somehow have something to do with my dad struggling with depression for so long? I shared what I had learned about these stuck, confused, suffering spirits with him and asked if he thought that perhaps a shamanic healing could help him feel better. "I'm willing to do that," he replied with a smile.

I contacted Tim Cope, the teacher at a workshop I had attended, and he suggested that he and Dad prepare for the experience with a few discussions via phone. Then Mom and I went with Dad to Tim's home for the actual ceremony, and I was glad we did. Going into a stranger's darkish basement filled with curious sacred objects to have a shamanic healing might not be all that reassuring without a trusted companion.

Tim was gracious and charming, making sure Dad was comfortable as he lay on the floor on some cushions, with my mother and I close by. Tim asked me if I would drum for him while he called his helping spirits, making me glad that I had followed my desire to learn to drum. To be able to participate in this way felt like a huge blessing to me.

After a couple of preliminary questions, Tim asked, in a strong and emphatic voice: "Joel, do you want to be healed?"

Dad responded with an inaudible mumble.

"I didn't hear that, Joel," Tim said, even more loudly. "Let me repeat my question: Do you want to be healed?"

Dad coughed. "Ah . . . yes . . . *yes,*" he finally replied.

"Okay, I heard you that time, Joel," Tim said with a broad grin. "Now let's get started."

I was surprised by the exchange. We'd been planning this visit for weeks and had driven three hours to get to Tim's home. Wasn't it obvious that Dad wanted to be healed? After hearing Tim's question and Dad's initial hesitancy, however, I realized how critical this question was, how important it was for my father to state his desire for healing. *And* how important it was for the healer not to be overzealous. If we aren't sure that we want to be healed, then our intention isn't clear. And shamanic work that isn't empowered by intention can either be a complete waste of time, or can have only temporary effects. I wondered how clear my dad's intention really was. Did he believe he deserved to be healed—to feel really good?

Tim began calling each of his spirits in a poetic and beautiful way—which I won't relate here, as it's his sacred work. When he indicated he was ready, I began to drum for him so that he could journey to another world to receive the healing instructions to help my father. I was nervous as I held the drum, hoping I was up to the task. I felt so happy to be able to contribute in this meaningful way.

When the healing work was complete, Tim indicated that I should stop drumming. Dad, who had fallen asleep, awoke with a start. Tim shared that, on his journey, he had been led back to the burning apartment in New York in which my grandmother had died. She (or her spirit) was still there in that burning room. *And she wasn't the only one stuck there.* A part of my Dad's soul was also stuck in that room. Tim had retrieved it and returned it to him. Tim also acted as a psychopomp—someone who facilitates the transitioning of dead souls—for my grandmother's spirit. He explained it like this to my dad: "My spirit helpers took your mom by the hand and escorted her lovingly to a place where she can be free from suffering and be healed."

Hearing this was incredibly moving. In fact, the whole experience made both my mother and me teary. I suddenly realized why it was so important that we had come. My parents told Tim that they'd never even had a funeral for my grandmother. "We were so young and in shock and really didn't know what to do," Mom explained. "And Lee hadn't wanted a funeral; she wanted her body to be donated to science." Tim had us all stand behind Dad, supporting him— literally, having his back—and when he was ready, we helped him push his mother's spirit into a virtual boat and send it symbolically out of this reality and into the next.

About six weeks after our visit to Tim, I was gifted with one of the most vivid and incredible night dreams I've ever had. Dad's mother came to visit me. She looked slender and elegant, her dark hair in soft waves, wearing red lipstick. I could feel her exuberant spirit. She was clearly in a heavenly place, happily sitting beneath an idyllic apple tree with my grandfather. She was so real and so palpable. I sobbed for joy and from the overwhelming compassion I sensed coming from her. I felt sure that Tim and his spirits had helped her to transcend.

Grandmother Lee approached me and said: "Sarah, I am so proud of you for writing these books and doing the work you are doing. I was a lot like you!" At this point, not wanting to wake Mark with my crying, I snuck out of bed, still in a sort of twilight state, and crept into my healing room. I curled up on the floor next to my altar under a blanket and shut my eyes, willing myself back into the dream. My grandmother returned immediately: "Sarah, I struggled so much and all I ever wanted to do was relieve suffering, just like you! I saw so much pain and I could feel it, just as you can. Keep going! You are doing good work!"

All I could do was say thank you over and over through my tears. Her dream visit came at a time when I desperately needed this boost—this encouragement from a kindred spirit to keep working on my writing and to stay the course. I crawled back into bed, spent from crying and so grateful.

CHAPTER 19

Everything Is Alive

Surely it is cruel to cut down a very fine
tree! Each dull, dead thud of the axe
hurts the little green fairy
that lives in its heart

Beatrix Potter, *The Fairy Caravan*

I am sitting in a beautiful spot on a hillside
in rural California at another Foundation
for Shamanic Studies workshop. There is an
enormous boulder beside me covered in soft,
thick, green moss. Through an exercise, I am
able to open up a conversation with it—a portal
of communication with this stone. It has a *lot* to
say. It isn't speaking out loud, however; instead,
I can hear its voice through my heart. I begin by
asking it what it has to teach me. Its response is
completely surprising.

"You should have seen the Gold Rush and all
of the horrible things people did to each other
in their lust for money. Just awful. I'm so happy
here in this place; it's *so* beautiful. If there is
one thing we stones are, it is patient." The stone

164

laughs, then asks: "Can you remove all the moss covering me? I love it when I can feel the warm rays of the sun on me."

I oblige the jolly stone. It laughs and carries on the whole time I am scraping off the moss with another stone. It is full of advice for me as well: "Love is a give-and-take—it's all about giving and receiving," suggesting that love is inherently reciprocal. And it offers career advice: "You could help people with their homes and the objects in them. You have a talent for that. It could be healing."

After three hours together, it is time for me to leave and we say our goodbyes. As I walk away, I have a sudden deeper realization that the world is not the way I once thought it was.

On the trail back to my room, returning from my new stone friend, I see the thousands of stones along the path—both large and small—and I am overwhelmed by the need to be polite. Hello, hello, hello! Good evening! Hope you are well. Oh, sorry; didn't mean to step on you so hard. And suddenly I truly know in my heart what I have been trying to comprehend in my mind——that *everything that is, is alive*. But how, I wonder, can I move through the world now that I know this?

As I walk along, surrounded by my new friends, I recall the words of Madeleine L'Engle in her book *A Wrinkle in Time*: "I don't understand it any more than you do, but one thing I've learned is that you don't have to understand things for them to be."

When I returned home later that week, I found that it wasn't just the stones that were alive; everything in my house was alive as well. How could I honor all of it and see what it needed or wanted? How could I get to know and honor each item? I began to understand how important it was to release and thank objects that no longer served me, so they could feel wanted by and useful to someone else, or so they could move forward in their own evolution to be recycled into something new.

I began to let go of even more of my possessions—things that had stopped giving me delight, things that felt heavy when I looked at them. A few T-shirts, suits, full-length ball gowns, and stacks and stacks of self-help books that I'd joyfully plowed through in the years preceding my sabbatical.

As I divested myself of clutter, I thanked each item for its service and then blessed it as I released it—to Goodwill, to the recycling bin, to the garbage, to a friend. Thank you. May you find a good home! Blessings! As I let go of more and more layers, I felt better and better. I found that I could appreciate and engage with the things that remained. Thank you, wonderful salad bowl! I'm grateful for you, beloved grey sweater jacket!

A week passed. It was November and, while idling at a stoplight downtown, I saw an enormous evergreen tree on a flatbed truck bound for our downtown square for the holidays. I felt the presence of this tree so strongly. It was as if I were seeing a dear friend rolling down the highway in an open casket. *Why do we do that?* Why do we destroy or sacrifice trees like that for our own celebration? Then I softened, wondering if perhaps it was an honor to be placed there to be admired. Maybe the tree wanted this as well. It was so confusing. I wept in my car, feeling like a stranger in my own city. It felt as if I knew too much—and yet not enough.

And I had yet another lesson to learn about this totally alive world I had discovered. I had to learn about the leaving of it. And the teaching came from an unexpected source

Our eleven-year-old pug Buttercup's tongue seemed to be hanging out more than usual. At first, we thought it was just something adorable about pugs as they age, but then we started to notice a growth on Buttercup's lip that extended under her tongue and began to erode her soft palate. She didn't seem to be in any pain—or if she was, she wasn't letting on. The vet, however, told us she was dying. I felt wracked with angst, wondering how I could help her. If her condition became more painful, how could we relieve her suffering?

A few days later, I was gifted with a dream. Buttercup was approaching a gigantic birth canal and womb. In a wacky, weird dream way, it was my womb, too. And the only way I could help her get back up into the womb was to relax. She was making her way (backward) up this canal. When she finally got back into the womb, she was filled (as was I) with a kind of ecstasy that permeated every single cell. Pure bliss. A holy climax of sorts.

The message to me: Buttercup doesn't need my help to die. She knows very well how to make this journey. In fact, this return trip will bring her so much joy and pleasure that it will be nothing short of amazing. I had it all wrong. *Death is nothing but a joyful return.* To help her, I just needed to relax. I scribbled in my journal: "Return to the womb or death is instinctual and brings great joy; it's a journey we must take alone. It brings much joy if we allow it."

I relaxed around Buttercup. I slowed down. When we went on our walks, I could see how she, too, wanted to move more slowly. There was an old evergreen at the trailhead near our home where Butter always loved to pause, sometimes for what seemed like an inordinately long time. Now she lingered even longer. As she grew closer to death, it seemed that her pleasure in this world grew deeper and deeper. She sniffed and examined everything with great longing, curiosity, and patience. She seemed to be giving me instruction on how to live—to pay rapt attention and to soak it all in.

CHAPTER 20

Soul Retrieval

Inside us there is something that has no
name, that something is what we are.

José Saramago, *Blindness*

In near darkness, I'm lying on a thin yoga mat
on a wood floor, my eyes covered by a soft
wool scarf. A fellow shamanic student who is
also a fellow physician is endeavoring, with the
help of his spirit guides, to find my lost soul
parts so they can be returned to me. We're lying
parallel to each other, surrounded by other pairs
of student healers. The drumming carries him
away while I lie present and curious. What could
have been lost?

I suddenly notice that he's on his knees
hovering over me. He cups his hands together
and places them over my heart. I sense a strange
feeling like electricity or a gentle forcefield as
his hands connect to my chest. Using his breath
as a delivery device, he blows the found parts
of my soul back into me. As he does, I feel an
expanding sense of lightness and warmth that

begins in my chest and spreads outward. The drumming rolls to a close and I slowly sit up.

He quietly shares in a rumbly whisper that my first missing soul part appeared to him as a babushka doll—those nested, hand-painted Russian dolls also known as *matryoshkas*. And there was a second soul piece that appeared as a leather-bound journal with a bear on its cover that was sitting on a desk.

Our instructor indicates that it is for me to decipher why those parts of my soul had fled or what they represented—with my spirits' help. So I embark on a shamanic journey that afternoon to find out what those parts of my soul represent so I can welcome them back. I travel down my familiar gravelly tunnel to meet up with Mother Bear and learn more about these returned parts. Lo and behold, these colorful dolls un-nest themselves and become marvelous, loving, dancing babushka ladies. A whole row of them dances and merrily potters about. They tell me that they are the mothering parts of me who enjoy cooking and caring for my family, being a nurturer, and bustling around the kitchen making wonderful things to eat.

In the shamanic view of the world, our souls represent our essence, our life force. We are conceived whole, with our souls intact. As we live our lives, certain situations, traumas, encounters, or experiences may cause parts of our souls to leave us to avoid a painful experience. You may even surrender a part of your soul voluntarily, offering it to another out of love or compassion.

Without those parts of our souls, however, we're not fully ourselves, not fully actualized. Shamanic practitioners know how to seek and retrieve these missing soul parts and ask them if they're willing to return. When soul parts return to us, more of our life force returns. According to many elder shamans, soul loss is the most widespread cause of disease on the planet.

So the marvelous, rosy-cheeked mommas I met on my shamanic journey were sending me an important message. Maybe I'd needed to leave medicine because I longed for *time to be a mother*. For many years, I'd longed to nurture, love, and care for my children, and to make my house a home. My babushka soul fragment probably fled, I intuited, during medical school and residency, when I realized I'd have to forego some of those nurturing and homemaking desires if I wanted to survive as a full-time medical resident-in-training. I found it ironic that the part of my soul that appeared as babushka dolls was retrieved by a fellow physician who was an extremely masculine male, as if this archetype were the very image with which I'd attempted to align in order to thrive in medicine.

In the weeks following that shamanic healing,

I discovered a spontaneous renewed interest in cooking healthy meals for my family. I reconnected with the joy of concocting wild meals, making them up freestyle from what I found in my refrigerator and pantry—a handful of cilantro, couscous, and (why not?) some raisins. Our kids were thrilled that I was more present to nurture them with the food I made, though they weren't all thrilled with the couscous.

But the matryoshka mommas weren't the only essential part of me that returned that day. It turned out that the leather-bound journal sitting on top of a desk represented my writer self. I reflected back and knew precisely where I had lost that part—in my freshman college literature course when I received a B+ for a paper on which I had worked diligently for weeks. My failure to get an A indicated to me that I wasn't meant to write. Now my writer self was back and that idea excited me.

CHAPTER 21

Sunglasses and Brass Knuckles

What makes the desert beautiful is that
somewhere it hides a well.

Antoine de Saint-Exupéry,
The Little Prince

Mark invited me to join his group in Arizona for a long weekend of healing. For several years now, Mark had been involved with an energy-healing class. This seemed like a perfect opportunity to understand what he'd been doing with his group and to deepen our connection with each other.

As we were preparing to leave, I asked Mark what I could expect to happen during the weekend. His response was that it was really hard to explain. I knew his group didn't do shamanic healing in the way I understood it. They didn't call upon specific loving and compassionate spirits by name, as I have learned to do. Instead, they used energy to heal, but he didn't seem able to explain what that actually meant. I understood

174

his challenge—a lot of these experiences are difficult to put into words.

We ate lunch at a tiny roadside diner and, as we headed back to the car, I counted dozens of vultures swirling in vortices above our heads in the thermals rising off the desert floor. Vultures are wild sanitizers, Nature's clean-up crew. I sensed a lot of healing was about to happen.

Organ Pipe National Park, near the Mexico-Arizona border, was unlike other deserts I had seen before. The land was hilly and dotted with glorious, huge, multilimbed cacti reaching skyward. At the visitor's center, Mark and I were totally taken with the educational displays. They had wonderful natural specimens of feathers, skulls, and scat. We lost track of time. Finally, one of the organizers' assistants came looking for us because we were two hours late. We hastily drove to the camping area and leapt out of the car to find the session already underway.

Sitting on lawn chairs in a circle under a temporary shelter from the blistering sun was a group of a dozen adults with an average age of forty-five to fifty-five. Mark and I were embarrassed to be late, knowing that it was a sacred circle we were entering. We joined the group as quietly as possible.

A discussion was underway in which the participants reported what had been going on in their lives over the last several months. The leader was engaging in what I immediately recognized as "brass knuckles" coaching—a form of coaching in which clients make themselves completely vulnerable and the coach focuses immediately on their greatest fears. It can feel a little like soul surgery *sans* anesthesia. My life-coaching mentor, Martha Beck, also calls this highly uncomfortable method of transformation the "wrecking ball" approach. I personally prefer velvet gloves.

Soon it was Mark's turn. "Well, I feel as if I haven't gotten much clearer. I'm still working on myself and haven't made much progress. I know I still have a lot of work to do," he said, grinning sheepishly.

The leader, who was wearing ominous-looking mirrored aviator sunglasses, immediately launched into Mark. "That's *always* your story, isn't it, Mark? Nothing is happening. Right?" He smiled. Yikes! This felt cultish.

But Mark didn't get defensive or freak out. He just looked calmly back at the leader, chuckled quietly, and said: "Yeah, I guess it is."

"Cool!" Sunglasses said, almost gleefully, as if to say: "Alrighty then. You're owning your shit. This is good news. Now let's move on to the next person."

Frankly, I wasn't loving this process, but it wasn't about me. And I must admit that I was feeling a little protective of Mark, because he seemed to have surrendered so completely to Sunglasses. If Mark loved personal transformation as much as it seemed he did, why hadn't he talked to me about it? Sometimes it seemed as if I hardly knew this man I'd been living with for twenty-plus years.

Then suddenly it was my turn.

"Well, hi. I'm Sarah," I began, "and I'm thankful to have been invited into this circle by my husband Mark, and I'm eager to learn and participate."

"Cool!" Sunglasses said.

Phew! I'd survived round one.

After these introductions, the group worked together on each individual. Each person's healing session took from one to two hours. Sunglasses prompted the students to ask questions of whoever was in the hot seat, and guided them to send healing energies in particular ways.

Each client selected the place in which they wanted to receive healing. One man with metastatic cancer chose an area full of dying cacti and scrubby brush. A mother-to-be chose an area that, we discovered midhealing, included a nest of owlets high up on a saguaro cactus limb. As her healing began, the owlets started to cry, which seemed to be a direct teaching about the demanding responsibilities of becoming a mother. Each place chosen seemed to hold perfect metaphors for the person who chose it.

Finally, after a few days of this, it was time for the group to work on Mark. It was roughly midday and the sun was high. We followed him to the spot he'd chosen—an exposed plateau. He was then instructed to lie down on a tarp spread out for protection against sharp, pointy cactus spines. Then—surprise—I was asked to lie down next to him. I reluctantly complied. The group stood above us and stared at us intently. As I squinted into the sun at the faces above us, they smiled and a few nodded their heads in apparent encouragement.

After a long silence, Sunglasses looked out at the group: "Hey, do you guys see what I'm seeing? They're mirror images of each other. Their bodies are identical." More people nodded.

Now wait a minute, I thought. Mark is six foot four and I'm five foot six. He is long and lithe and I'm slightly more sturdy, like Popeye. After a bit more staring, Sunglasses said: "No offense, Sarah, and I'm not sure just how to put this, but you're not—let's just say . . ." And then he alluded to the fact that I'm rather flat-chested. Where was this going? Was he going for a deeper metaphor about us being mirrors for each other. I silently reminded myself that I was there for Mark and that I could simply disregard anything Sunglasses said.

Silence fell again. The whole group continued

to stare at us in the ninety-degree heat. It occurred to me that lying on the desert floor in the midday sun was probably putting us both into an altered state.

"Tell us about what you want to heal, Mark," Sunglasses said.

"I'd like to work on my breathing. I just feel sometimes as if I can't breathe, as if I'm suffocating." Mark has sleep apnea. He uses a device at night that helps, but he hates having to be plugged into it in order to sleep. He'd like to be free of the problem.

After a pause, Sunglasses resumed: "Okay. Sarah and Mark, I'm wondering if you'd be willing to do something for us. Sarah, will you get up on top of Mark?"

WTF? I had come to this desert. I had sweated. I had slept in a tent on the extremely lumpy desert floor. I had observed the brass-knuckles coaching action for a couple days. And now he wanted me to lie on top of my husband in front of everyone?

Just as I was thinking this, Mark indicated with a shrug and nod that it was totally fine with him. As I picked myself up off the tarp and positioned myself above him, I continued silently reminding myself that I was here for Mark. Then I gently lowered myself onto him, not sure what was coming next. Suddenly, I was laughing inside. Was I "on top"—too dominant—in our relationship? Was this the metaphor?

We smiled silently at each other as I turned my head and rested it on his chest. Body to body, I could feel Mark's familiar heartbeat. It was high noon, and I was lying atop my husband on a tarp in the desert near the Mexican border while a group of people I barely knew stared down at us.

"How's that, Mark?" Sunglasses interrupted the silence. "Can you breathe *now?*"

Mark smiled and chuckled softly. "Yes, this actually feels good."

At this point, I was just glad that I hadn't been identified as the immediate cause of Mark's suffocation. Then, more silence. As we continued to lie together—quietly breathing, connected—I thought: This is vulnerability. This is being willing to do whatever it takes, to be laid bare and allow our relationship of twenty-one years to be examined. This surrender to each other, to the group, to the Universe is simply a way of saying we are *willing*. Whatever happens after this doesn't really matter.

Then, to my relief, I was asked to roll off Mark. After input from the group, the session wrapped up with an assignment from Sunglasses, who told Mark to initiate pillow fights with me—metaphorically and literally—to elicit more fun between us. My job was simply to go along with the fun. Simple enough, right? It seemed Sunglasses had uncovered a pattern—Mark was too serious around me.

Afterward, Mark and I did have some awkward pillow fights, with lots of laughs. Though our desert stay was a strange and nonlogical experience, it most definitely brought us closer together. Mark continued to use his sleep apnea machine at night, but the air between us seemed easier to breathe—for both of us.

Maybe even more important, I learned that Mark truly and deeply longed to shift his own patterns, just as badly as I wanted to shift mine. And he was willing to go into the desert and endure guys in sunglasses with brass knuckles in order to do it. He wanted to awaken and blossom like a lotus, just as I did, and he was willing to be vulnerable in front of a crowd (even if not always at home). This surprised me and cracked me open. I was now aware of a part of him that he hadn't often revealed to me. And I loved him more.

Postdesert, I invited Mark to take a journey with me and asked if I could journey to request a healing for him. He'd been noticing a lack of joy in his heart and a feeling of being "less than." He agreed.

We lay down next to each other on the bedroom floor with my phone playing the drumbeat. I briefly explained the simple procedure to go to the Lower World. Mark went in search of an animal totem for himself, and I went to request a healing for him. As I arrived in the Lower World, a single friendly dolphin showed up. I explained that Mark wasn't feeling "good enough" and didn't feel joy in his heart. I was brought to a whole pod of dolphins in shallower water, where we joined in a circle. The dolphins began to swim faster and faster, stirring up cloudy sediment from the deep—Mark's hurt and pain. Then they began to emit green smoke from their hearts, which drifted and turned the murky water crystal clear.

I thanked them and hugged each dolphin. Then they gave me a ride back to the beach, where Mother Bear met me. I fell into a hug, so happy that I had tears in my eyes. Mark and I both returned to the bedroom floor from our journeys and quietly wrote down a few notes. I could feel a sweetness and peace settling over both of us.

I thanked Mark for letting me journey for him and told him what a really beautiful thing it had been. Then I told him about the dolphins.

Mark smiled gently, almost shyly. "Mine was confusing," he said. "I saw a lot of different images of different animals shapeshifting, but it was amazing and really peaceful."

Our eyes were softer, our hearts bigger, our connection deeper as we shared our experiences. I felt so much more connected to Mark, and I knew this work was helping me. Helping us.

CHAPTER 22

Emergency Sabbatical

In order to understand the world, one has
to turn away from it on occasion.

Albert Camus, *The Myth of Sisyphus*

Mark is walking through an apocalyptic
landscape; I follow about ten paces behind
him. He suddenly encounters a raging river. As
he nears the river's edge, I begin to cringe and
start to shout: *"No!"* The edge of the river is
unstable. The ground beneath his feet crumbles
and he plunges into the rapids and disappears.
Without thinking, I dive in after him. Only then,
when it's too late, do I see my folly. I shouldn't
have impulsively leaped in after him.

I wake up. It was just a dream.

Days later, Mark came home from work
and declared: "I think I need an emergency
sabbatical." He wanted to go on a forty-two-
day intensive vision quest in Montana that was
being run by a friend, but he wasn't sure it was
possible.

"How good are you willing to let it get?" I asked, posing the life-coachy question that I used to help me when faced with similar options.

Mark was worried. "I don't know what they'll say at work."

The proposed adventure was only six weeks away, which meant that there wasn't much time to shuffle his patients around so that other doctors could care for them while he was away. Mark looked frustrated and torn. "It can't hurt to ask," I offered.

A few days later, Mark got a thumbs up from work. Before he left for Montana, we went on a weekend get-away we had previously planned—a romantic trip to the north shore of Lake Superior. When we arrived at the resort, we decided that kayaking on the lake would be fun. We hired a guide, sharing him with a well-coiffed and warm forty-something Chicago couple who were also staying at the resort.

We headed down to the rocky beach with lightweight kayaks and their skirts on a sunny, late-July day. We threw on life jackets, got a quick lesson from the energetic guide on how to paddle, and launched. We had all kayaked before and, although the lake's surface wasn't entirely flat, the waves were small and soft. As we moved out onto the lake, there was something about the scale of this body of water that I found mildly terrifying. It was more ocean than lake. I was finding it hard to keep up.

We went north first to see the mouth of a river with its picturesque low cliffs, then made our way south, aiming for the sea caves. The shoreline changed from low sand beaches to three-story-high walls of red stone that dropped precipitously into the water. There was nowhere to go ashore anymore. Then the wind picked up a bit and there was some mild chop, but the day remained sunny. We began to see small caves and stone cliffs arching over the water that we could paddle beneath. It was stunning but also eerie.

Finally, we arrived near an opening in the rocky cliff, all bobbing in our kayaks. Our guide wanted to show us something. He demonstrated how to maneuver the slim kayak into the narrow little cave and get a look inside, then how to back out by pushing with the paddle.

I went first, paddling slowly into the little inlet of the cave. Inside, it was dark and filled with jagged rocks. It felt a little claustrophobic and smelled damp and funky. I backed out and paddled out of the way for Mark, who went in next. He paddled in okay, but when he tried to back out, his kayak seemed to get stuck on the rocky bottom. The next thing I knew, he had capsized and was trying to wrangle his six-foot-four self out of the kayak. Suddenly, this fun, playful exploration became deadly serious.

Instantly, I remembered my recent dream and my impulsive desire to save Mark, to leap into the water after him. Shamans teach that night dreams can be incredibly important and, at times, can serve to alert us so we can avoid an undesireable outcome in "ordinary" reality.

I felt all of us panic. The water was viciously cold—cold enough to render you unconscious in fifteen to thirty minutes. And with the hundred-foot soaring walls of stone, there was no way to swim to land. The kayaks were skimpy—there was no way to take on a passenger—and Mark's was swamped with water. Our guide quickly became all business. "Mark, center yourself," he quietly commanded. "You're going to need to get back in the kayak."

I caught a glimpse of Mark's face as he attempted to orient himself. He looked as if he had seen a horrible ghost, as if he'd aged fifteen years in ten seconds. Did he hit his head on the rocks as well? I tried to stay calm, so I wouldn't add to his anxiety. Thank God the guide was steady.

Mark quickly scrambled to stabilize the kayak while the guide helped from his own. Mark finally slipped back into the kayak, but it was still half-submerged and unable to float. Mark was soaked, freezing, and pale as the moon. What the hell had we been thinking coming out here? Mark could die. How far were we from a place where we could go ashore? A mile? Three?

The guide reached into his kayak and pulled out a packable down jacket that he handed over to Mark and told him to put on. Then he pulled out a pump and began furiously working it from his lap so that small geysers shot out of Mark's kayak. The rest of us watched silently. Then the guide made an irreverent reference to masturbation, and we all started laughing. Oh my God, it was a relief to laugh. I was so scared.

Mark's color started to come back and, with his kayak emptied, he was afloat once again. We pointed our kayaks back out into open water and began to paddle carefully and solemnly back along the shore beneath the red rock cliffs. I thought of my friend's brother, an experienced kayaker, who had gone out one beautiful after-noon for a paddle on this north shore just a few years before and never returned. This lake was as remorseless as it was mesmerizing. We finally hit the stony shore and hauled our kayaks out one by one. I had never been so happy to be off the water.

Riding back in the van, I felt a weird desire to hug and kiss our guide. If he hadn't been so prepared, Mark might not have survived. This seemed to have been another kind of initiation— for both Mark and me. I was also reminded of how precious Mark was to me, and was made newly aware of his absolute vulnerability.

· · ·

The time finally arrived for Mark to head for his emergency sabbatical on a mountainside in Montana. Like me, he was searching—wanting to realize his full potential and return to wholeness. I was excited for him.

Mark left fully stocked with headlamps and long woolen underwear. At the last minute, he even contemplated rolling up the fluffy, Greek lambs-wool rug from under our living room furniture to put in the back of his truck in case he needed it for warmth. Mark, like me, seemed to be struggling to let it all go.

Mark's vision quest included kundalini yoga, the yoga of awareness that focuses on awakening a potential primal energy lying coiled like a serpent at the base of the spine. It involved meditation, special breathing techniques, poses, and hours and hours spent in complete darkness and isolation in a yurt he'd make from twigs and black plastic.

While he was away, we weren't in contact much because his cell phone didn't work unless he climbed up pretty high on the mountain. At one point, however, about three weeks into the trip, he called. I could tell from his voice that things were not going well. When I asked how he was doing, he answered that he missed us and sometimes wished he were home.

Mark sounded really down—as if he was

actually contemplating coming home early. Instead of feeling supportive, however, I felt annoyed. I was completely overwhelmed with trying to deal with all the start-of-school anxieties, the new-student orientations and parent-teacher meetings. In a way, I would have absolutely loved it if he cut his vision quest short. But that was my selfish self. I ordered it to quiet down and I offered encouragement: "It won't be long and you'll be back home driving kids to soccer and hauling the garbage can to the curb. So take advantage of the time." I was in a dark metaphorical yurt of my own, and I wasn't feeling up to soothing souls.

Just before Mark left, I had asked him what he thought of getting a second dog. The last time he'd gone out of town for an extended period, I'd brought home the world's most irrepressible dog. I recall driving over the hill on the way to the shelter with the kids and wondering if I were doing the right thing. Then, at that very moment, a huge eagle soared over the hood of our car and the kids, knowing how attuned I was to the messages of animals, shouted and pointed it out. It felt like a sign—one that seemed to be confirmed when we arrived at the shelter and spotted a lithe and glossy black-brown dog with white socks and chest and a big smile. She reminded me of a hyperattentive border collie crossed with an overexcitable Irish setter.

"Spirit," as the shelter had named her in another burst of synchronicty, was a feisty, fun dog. As I began walking her off the leash in the woods, I found myself continually calling: "Come, Spirit, *come!*" to get her to return to me. One day, I just laughed out loud at the irony of it all. I think my helping spirits were having a pretty good time with me.

With Buttercup no longer around, however, Spirit had become anxious. I wondered if she would be calmer if she had another dog companion. When I asked Mark what he thought, he seemed resigned and told me to do what I thought best. He didn't say no, I told myself, and chose to interpret this as "Go ahead." So the kids and I piled into the car and drove to the animal shelter. I reminded them that we were only bringing home a new dog if it was the right dog for us.

When we arrived, we were introduced to Maximus, a highly anxious long-haired chihuahua who warmed up to us once we met in a private room. Maximus was highly sensitive. We were told he might not take kindly to males. I ignored this and pushed through. He was soft and snuggly. We brought him home.

Maximus slept under the covers in the crook behind my knee and liked to sit on top of my desk, watching me adoringly as I worked. The kids loved him, too, but George got a little scared when the dog bared its teeth as he gently approached. This all happened, of course, the week before I was to travel to West Virginia to teach medical students at Patch Adams's Gesundheit Institute.

Our fearless Mary Poppins-like sitter, Meghan, arrived to run the ship while I was gone and Mark was still off the grid in a yurt in Montana. She was eminently capable and continued smiling even when I explained that, the week before, I had added another dog to the family. If she was disappointed in my judgment, she didn't show it—which is why she was my favorite sitter. I left town feeling relaxed.

One night, there was a knock on my door in West Virginia. "Sarah, one of your kids is on the phone." I rushed to take the call, worried that something awful had happened. There was no cell service there, so a call on the house phone wasn't likely to be good news. It was Katherine; she sounded panicked. "Mom, it's Maximus; he's gone crazy! He only really likes *you*." It seemed that Maximus had staked himself out on a corner of our front stoop this wintry night and refused to budge. All approaches were met with ferocious growling, and Meghan had already been bitten once, albeit without major damage.

Meghan got on the line and voiced her concern that the dog would freeze if left outside overnight. I sat on the stairs in the Gesundheit hallway flooded with shame at having brought home this anxious, needy dog then leaving the next week. The kids were upset and even scared of Maximus, not sure that they wanted him back in the house. Suddenly, I remembered my friend Marta, a fierce dog advocate. I arranged for her to handle the situation. But I couldn't seem to stop beating myself up. It really devastated me to think that our love hadn't been enough to bring Maximus peace, and I worried that he'd never find a permanent home. To make matters worse, Meghan told me that, when they couldn't get through to me right away, they'd also tried Mark's cell phone in Montana, so he already knew about the dog debacle and was on his way home. Grab a fork; I was about to be served humble pie.

Mark got back just in time to pick me up at the airport after my return flight from West Virgina. I was so excited to see him again, sure that all that yoga, fresh air, and down time would have him feeling fantastic. When he got out of the car to grab my luggage, however, I barely recognized him. He had a full beard and had lost thirty, maybe even forty, pounds. He had always been slim, but now he looked gaunt and hollow—not adorable Gandhi skinny but deathly skinny, as if he were being consumed by an alien parasite. We hugged and kissed briefly. He smelled musty and decaying, as if he not only *looked* half-dead but actually *was* half-dead.

I was scared and infuriated. How could Mark come back in this state? What the hell were they doing out there? Starving themselves to death? This was supposed to be his break, his chance to restore, to become more vital and healthy. Instead, he'd returned weakened and sickly. What was the point?

We drove solemnly down the freeway toward home. Even Mark's car smelled a little like death. I tried to conceal my aversion. We talked about practical, safe things like the kids and his drive back from Montana. He seemed down, almost depressed. I wasn't even sure how to begin to talk with him about it. I wasn't sure what he could handle right now. He didn't seem to have any awareness of how unwell he appeared, and he was so subdued that I felt as if I needed to go easy.

We stopped for dinner at a Chinese restaurant off the freeway and I finally asked him if he had found what he was looking for out there in Montana. I searched his face for answers. He paused and then said, with a bit of hesitation: "Yeah I did have a moment where it seemed as if something did happen when I was sitting in the darkness." I didn't push for details. Mark had always been a deeply private person, and I wanted to respect that.

Over the next weeks, I baked a lot of oatmeal cookies and cooked lots of family dinners. To my relief, Mark ate and returned to his normal physical condition pretty quickly. A new calmness and peacefulness seemed to arise in him. His smile returned. So did his sense of humor. He confessed that he'd secretly snuck maple syrup in to put on his bland quinoa porridge ration from the lean-to kitchen when he was half-starving from self-imposed dietary restrictions. A few months later, I could see that he was happier now than he had been before—more content.

Maybe sometimes we need to die a little bit in order to be reborn.

During a walk in the woods a few weeks later, I came across a pair of towering white pines enfolding each other in a perpetual, twisted, harmonious embrace. The two trunks seemed to be saying to me: You and Mark, you'll find a way. This partnership is rare and valuable. Cherish it.

CHAPTER 23

India Calling

Tourism may take us to "see the sights,"
but pilgrimage takes us for darshan,
the "beholding" of a sacred image
or a sacred place.

Diana L. Eck, *India: A Sacred Geography*

Being on "casual status" at the hospital after my sabbatical made me feel more anxious about money and how I'd pay for my continuing shamanic training—not to mention college for our four kids. When I asked my helping spirits how I could achieve financial independence, I was told to meditate.

Apparently, I needed to sit my anxiety-ridden self down in the lotus position. So I began to practice. I did it for a few days, but it was *really* hard. So I stopped. I preferred to move; so instead, I created my own wacky version of *shinrin-yoku*—a kind of a walking meditation and divination I'd devised after discovering and falling in love with the Japanese word, which means "forest bathing." I wandered slowly in the woods, focusing on open-ended questions and listening with my whole body for the answer.

When I felt lonely and disconnected, I asked: "How can I feel better today?" Birds calling back and forth to each other in the woods reminded me that I could pick up the phone and arrange to meet friends for coffee to help me feel less isolated in my new solo endeavor. When I asked how I could learn to love and accept myself, dying trees that had fallen over and were slowly decaying and disappearing into the forest floor made themselves known to me, and I saw how graceful they were in their simple surrender. Maybe I could be beautiful like that as well. I saw that I was dying, too—or at least parts of me were.

When I journeyed to ask (again!) how I could free myself from financial worries, the answer, once again, was to "sit on a lotus" (aka meditate). This time, my guides even showed me how. I was supposed to sit on the ground—legs crossed, back straight, palms resting open on my knees—and breathe. They showed me that having a straight back was important in order to line up all of my energy centers. It was rather embarrassing that the spirits had to tell me this, not once, but several times. Clearly, they were being firm with me; I wanted to honor them.

As I sat, my mind raced with ideas, thoughts, lists. At first, I allowed myself a pad of paper to jot things down. I often got insights I wanted to capture or was reminded of mundane stuff like the kids' dental appointments. Eventually, over several weeks and months, I experienced glimpses of bliss. Surprise! I'd drop quickly into a sweet space of ease and effortlessness. Sometimes, it lasted just a few minutes. Other times, it lasted longer. It kept getting easier and, over time, fewer thoughts came to disturb me. It seemed as if the less I needed it to be blissful, the more likely it was to be so. On days when I missed meditation, I was aware of my own struggle for peace and calm. On days when I meditated, my disposition seemed sweeter, my patience greater, and my heart more expansive.

Having time to meditate or wander in the forest was a revelation to me. But being on "casual status" at the hospital was also an uncomfortable kind of limbo. People asked me if I was ever going back, to which I responded: "Oh, I'm *still* a doctor. I'm just on 'casual status.' My partners can call me if they need me to come in and help." It felt as if I were trying to reassure myself as well as them. I felt as if I were convincing myself that I was still needed.

When my partners actually *did* call me in to work occasionally, however, I experienced deep dread. Returning to visit friends at work was wonderful, but going back to work at my microscope felt terribly stifling. I was caught between two lives. I wanted to let people at the hospital know that I was still doing something meaningful, but even I wasn't exactly sure where it was all heading. So much of what *was* happening took place during my shamanic journeys and coaching sessions. Being in Nature was profoundly healing. I was receiving helpful messages from loving spirits. But how could I begin to tell them about that?

I was still finding it hard to let go of the solidity of my medical career. It was something people could comprehend and admire. But being a life coach or shamanic healer? In the minds of many, I imagined, that was an occupation on a par with being a New Age cult member. The chasm of understanding often felt unbridgeable.

In my overcrowded and jumbled inbox, I noticed an email from a local yoga studio. They were sponsoring a trip to India for an event called the *Kumbh Mela*. An informational session was scheduled in a few weeks. The email told of an extraordinary adventure—not just a mere trip.

> When the celestial bodies, planets, and stars all align with perfection, it creates a potent and fertile field of spiritual power in Allahabad where the three holiest rivers meet. Every twelve years, pilgrims, wise beings, and saints converge in this

powerful spot to unite and pray with one heart to remove fear and suffering from the planet. This sacred pilgrimage has been occurring for millennia.

I investigated online and discovered that the Kumbh Mela is a Hindu pilgrimage—a long journey to a sacred place as an act of religious devotion. This particular one is equivalent to doing one hundred typical pilgrimages. It's the Superbowl of Hindu pilgrimages. My inner over-achiever's interest was piqued.

The Kumbh Mela is rooted in a Hindu mythological text, the *Bhagavata Purana*. In the myth, there's a battle in which light and dark, or good and evil forces, fight over a jug of goo called the nectar of immortality (*amrita*). During this tug of war, the jug accidentally spills and the nectar lands in several spots, one of which is the Ganges river near Allahabad, where the most famous Kumbh Mela takes place. When the nectar spilled into the Ganges, the water became infused with sacred power. The river literally *became* amrita, the nectar of immortality.

Every twelve years, during astrologically predictable periods, the Ganges is believed to transform, once again, into an intense power spot, where the veil between this world and the spirit worlds becomes thin. So for thousands of years, people have been coming to dip in the river at this spot to be blessed and to have their karma (or sins) washed away.

Washing away lifetimes of bad karma, or the spiritual impact of my previous not-so-great choices, sounded sublime. Could a dip in the river help lighten my load?

I forwarded the email to my friend Suzi, hoping to convince her to check it out with me. Getting to India also involved shelling out five thousand dollars, and spending that kind of cash felt really irresponsible in our current circumstances. Our emergency savings had dwindled to a new low. The trip made no logical sense. Could I even swing leaving our four kids and Mark behind for twenty-one days?

One night, safely ensconced in bed, I watched the documentary *Shortcut to Nirvana*, shot in 2001 at the last Kumbh Mela in Allahabad, which had been attended by sixty million people. *Shortcut*'s title plays on the fact that, spiritually speaking, the Kumbh Mela pilgrimage is viewed by many as a fast track to immortality. In other words, if you complete this pilgrimage successfully, instead of being reborn into this world again when you die, you won't have to reincarnate, but will instead be freed, released from suffering.

Shortcut's filmmakers followed some American pilgrims around the Mela to get their perspective on the whole experience. I listened carefully, as a way to help myself decide whether I wanted to go or not. Some pilgrims reported being overwhelmed by the sights and sounds, saying it was kind of awful. This was my first hint that the experience might not be all chai and marigolds.

Some of the *sadhus*, or holy men, portrayed in the film seemed to be tricksters. They did sketchy, wild, yogic feats like stretching their penises around sticks (run to your computer now and find that video online!). In yoga, as in all spiritual traditions, there are subgroups that value asceticism, foregoing pleasures in life and even enduring severe pain in order to seek enlightenment. I seriously began to wonder what any of this had to do with my own journey.

I also uncovered a few unsavory bits about the Kumbh Mela. In 1954, there was a stampede in which 854 people died. The crowds then weren't nearly as large as those predicted for 2013. Estimates ranged from fifty to eighty million people over the six-week period. If things got out of hand, it seemed that calamity and tragedy would be certain.

On the day of the informational meeting, it poured buckets. There were perhaps thirty of us sitting in a circle on folding metal chairs in a yoga studio. The speaker was a lively, slender, glowing woman in her forties who was dressed all in white and wearing mala beads—long strands of beads made out of dried seed pods used, much like a rosary, for tracking repeated mantras or prayers. Even her outfit was strangely promising. In Duluth, *nobody* wears all white—not even in August.

"Isn't the rain wonderful?" she bubbled as she began. "You know, in India, rain is considered a very good sign—a blessing, a portent of good things to come." Could this precipitation be a positive signal from the Universe?

"What we are planning here is a spiritual journey," she continued. "Our group will do meditation practices and pray for the earth. If we do this, if we *all* come together *in this time and in this place,* the entire world will benefit." In other words, if we each did a good job at this Kumbh Mela, the next twelve years would be auspicious, or at least would be better than if we had not.

The speaker then told us about the significance of the geography: "In this spot in Allahabad, there are three rivers—two visible and the other mythical. Where we'll camp, the three merge to become the Ganges." When I heard this description, I felt a tremendous inner thrill. Suddenly, I knew this pilgrimage was for me.

I had seen these rivers merging before. I had sketched this symbolic confluence in my journal several different times, months before I ever knew anything about a Kumbh Mela. In my journeys with Alice, I often stood on a spit of land between two rivers, which merged to become one. This spit of land is where I always found Alice waiting for me. The larger river is very deep, powerful, and still; it had long been a metaphor for how to create what I desire from a place of stillness. I felt a weird knowingness pour over me—an understanding that *this trip is what's next.*

I drove home and confessed hesitantly to Mark that I had a feeling this really *was* the trip for me. I was relieved when his eyes kindly registered his understanding. "Sounds good," he said, effectively giving me the thumbs up. We had given up arguing over trivial expenses in the last two decades, but big expenses like this still required two "yesses" to act on and only one "no" to veto.

I hadn't anticipated feeling so strongly drawn to traveling to India on a pilgrimage. Sure, exotic travel fascinated me, and I admired Ghandi (who doesn't?). But this adventure felt less like Condé Nast and more like *Into the Wild.*

With Mark's approval, I mailed in my five-hundred-dollar deposit. The Kumbh Mela was eighteen months away; I could still bail out. I continued to mention India half-heartedly to Suzi. But as Suzi herself often says: "If you mention something to someone more than three times, you're trying to control them."

Word.

CHAPTER 24

Laid by the Universe

In the attitude of silence the soul finds
the path in a clearer light, and what is
elusive and deceptive resolves itself
into crystal clearness.

Mahatma Gandhi, *The Way to God*

In the meantime, fascinated by everything I
was encountering with the spirits, I returned
to a more advanced Foundation for Shamanic
Studies workshop out in California. We were
asked to merge, spiritually, with a particular part
of the earth. To be effective, a shaman must learn
to work in harmony with all of creation. As I'd
learned from my experience with the boulder, the
earth has knowledge she can impart.

As I lay on the floor, eyes covered, in the near
darkness, I set my intention. As I merged, I began
to have a feeling I recognized—ecstasy, a pure
pleasure flooding my body. It grew and grew. It
felt as if the ley lines, or mystical pathways of
energy running through my body, were being
crammed with so much love and power and joy

that they broke open again and again to make more space. I was being broken open so I that could allow more of this love and bliss to fill me. The feeling just kept building and building, with no end in sight.

As I experienced this sensation, I simultaneously began to wonder if it were okay to be having it. I always liked to keep one foot firmly planted in "reality." Was it weird to be having this extremely pleasurable experience? It felt like those most intense moments of love-making when you don't dare move because you want to hold on to the ecstasy for a few more moments before it peaks and abruptly dissipates. Now, however, I was free of the anxiety that the feeling would end.

Eventually, the call-back drumming sequence sounded, and I had to return my consciousness to the room. I wasn't sure what had just happened to me. We closed the circle and headed for supper, instructed not to share our experiences until later in class. I noticed that many participants seemed to be glowing and happy.

I wondered about the purpose of this pleasure and whether there was something I was supposed to be doing about it. When we were asked to share our experiences with a partner, I told her that it felt as if I were getting laid by the Universe. We laughed hard. "That sounds pretty nice!" she said. She had a totally different experience but one that was also joyful.

By the time I returned from this training, I had learned many different healing methods—soul retrieval, extraction, animal spirit retrieval, and more. I was becoming more comfortable offering healing work to others and began inviting my existing and former coaching clients to experience it. I asked people simply to bring a small gift as payment—flowers or something they had made. One of my shamanic teachers had admonished against charging money when we began. "You need to find out if your work is *effective,*" she cautioned. "You will know when it's time to charge." That resonated deeply with me. I was feeling less anxious about money than ever before. It seemed as if everything we needed was being provided. Looking back over my life, I realized that it always had been, but now I could see that with a greater clarity.

Over time, I have worked with people with various challenges—a sense of deep emptiness following the death of a mother, chronic medical conditions, physical ailments like lyme disease, fear over financial concerns, confusion over what their highest path in life was, and depression. When I work with these clients, I light my candle and call my helping spirits using my rattle. I invariably feel supported, and I ask them to help my client. My helping spirits appear and make recommendations and share healing, love, and wisdom. The process of communication with the spirits reminds me of the process of making a diagnosis under the microscope when things are not so straightforward. You almost have to listen for the cells to tell you if they are malignant or benign. This is the soft, intuitive part—the art— of medicine.

I remember once when I correctly identified a rare tumor in an unusual site on a tiny fragment of tissue on a frozen section. My partner marveled later, after everyone had consulted, and asked me how I had known what it was. When I tried to recreate the moment, all I could say was that the diagnosis popped into my head. And I knew I'd been helped by that voice many times. In the case of the spirits, however, the communication was now more intentional. And my healing work continued to prove to me that it was valid.

A client with hepatitis reported that her serum markers for liver inflammation were significantly reduced days after our shamanic work together. Another reported her child-like joy had returned and that she'd been smiling a lot more. One said that she was surprised at how easily she'd been able to stop her habitual use of marijuana; she hadn't smoked for three months. Another said he'd been "uncharacteristically calm and loving and felt remarkably well." Bit by bit, reinforced by these experiences, I began to build a trusting relationship with myself and with my spirits. If

I could be an effective conduit, and my clients truly wanted to be well, the spirits would heal them.

Some seemed to experience almost miraculous results. One client reported how a shamanic healing with me had marked a pivotal point in her life. Ever since that healing, she said, her law practice had taken off, and she'd achieved her dream of owning a horse. "I've lost fifty pounds and life is beautiful," she wrote. "I continue my work, in all its mystery, but I am so grateful for my session with you." This is the kind of feedback that tells me I am on the right path.

It is hard, however, when I don't hear back from clients or when they occasionally report that they aren't sure that anything has changed. When I journey to Alice or other spirits to ask about these individual situations, I am often told to mind my own business or that more has yet to be revealed. Sometimes, I even worry that I am getting in the way. When I question my spirits' information during a healing, they respond by asking if I trust them—to which the only answer is "yes." And each time—no matter how odd the information I share—somehow it seems that clients connect with it and can see how it fits in with their intention. I have to remind myself that, while I am responsible for the effort, the outcome is really between my clients and the spirits.

Experience by experience, I am growing more

and more dedicated to this way of the spirits. I can often see a person shift before my eyes, telling me that good things are happening. Most days aren't filled with "getting laid by the Universe" sort of bliss, however. Instead, I find a quiet and profound ecstasy in serving like this—even when I can't completely understand it. The exquisite beauty of working in this way *is* the understanding.

After one particularly difficult week, feeling thwarted and throttled by life, I realized that I desperately needed a retreat. Intrigued by Mark's vision quest—which, in the long term, seemed to have a positive effect on him—I devised a brief vision quest of my own at a hotel conveniently nearby. Doing a quest in the wild seemed too complicated. I didn't have time for six weeks in a yurt; school was about to start. An overnight would have to do. Besides, I got the weekend rate.

Mark was happy to cover the home base. As fasting seemed classic for a vision quest, I skipped breakfast that morning. Like other forms of deprivation, fasting is supposed to have the effect of helping you connect more deeply with the Divine. Who knows? I made it up as I went along.

I left home early Saturday morning, checked in at a flashy, recently refurbished hotel, and headed up to my room. Despite the lobby's polished appearance, however, as the elevator doors slid open, I saw that the upper floors felt tired. I was longing for beauty—the kind I knew I'd find in Nature. Could I find it here?

My room, like the hallway, didn't feel pristine or sacred to me *at all*. I carefully lit some cedar incense with the intention of clearing out the room's mustiness and inviting love and light to enter. I set up a small altar and rolled out my vintage sari quilt on the floor. Then I lay down, preparing to take a journey. That's when I noticed the artwork on the wall. It was an architectural rendering of the Taj Mahal. Most hotels in northern Minnesota are adorned with images of rugged Canadian Mounties encountering bears. The Taj? I did a double take.

I'm not sure what image could have been hanging there that could have made me feel more loved—or *more divinely supported*. It was as if the spirits were telling me that they were present, even in this remodeled, less-than-perfect, 1970s hotel room in Duluth.

I'd just recently gotten the thrilling news that a visit to the Taj Mahal had been added to the itinerary of the Khumb Mela pilgrimage. The Taj Mahal was a place I had been shown again and again on my visits with Alice to the Upper World. Though I generally crave speed and getting things done in a flash, my encounters with this structure in the spirit world had taught me that things worth creating take time, love, and a big dose of patience. After all, the magnificent monument had taken twenty-two years and an unfathomable amount physical force and power to complete.

Moreover, the building's purpose was a powerful one. It had been commissioned by the grief-stricken Shah Jahan in memory of his wife, who had died in childbirth. The Shah dreamed that those who entered the Taj Mahal would experience love and cosmic pardoning. His daunting project would take most of the rest of his life to complete. When I'm working on projects that take a lifetime—parenting my kids, building my marriage, being a friend and daughter—I try to remember the burnt naan bread, the exhausted people and elephants, and the long journey to completion of the Taj Mahal. And I remember that love was the reason it was all envisioned in the first place.

As I lay down on the hotel room floor and journeyed beneath the symbolic image of the Taj, I realized that what I *really* longed to do, more than a vision quest, was to complete the book I'd been working on. When I first started writing it, I was afraid to share some of my more personal stories, so I consulted Alice, asking her if my writing would serve others. How could I be sure that the words I wrote would not be misunderstood or, worse yet, cause injury?

In response to these concerns, Alice had taken me on a free fall into a pitch-black abyss. At first, this plunge scared the hell out of me. But then I looked to my side, and I saw and felt Alice falling alongside me, doing flips and twirls and laughing at me in a kindly way, letting me know that it was okay to let go. It was, after all, a free fall, and I couldn't know the outcome ahead of time. It was a risk, she was telling me. Enjoy! Gently, Alice informed me that I needed to learn to become comfortable with and even *relish* the experience of not knowing the outcome.

And I learned that I couldn't write when I was hungry. So I quickly decided to break my four-hour fast by ordering from room service and got to work putting the finishing touches on my second book. Starving myself had never been my strong suit.

CHAPTER 25

Saint Teresa

Union is as if in a room there were two
large windows through which the light
streamed in. It enters in different places,
but it all becomes one.

Teresa of Ávila, *Interior Castle*

The three-year program at the Foundation for
Shamanic Studies gave me a solid footing
for my healing work. I'd recently run across an
intriguing book cover with Teresa of Ávila, the
Spanish mystic and Roman Catholic saint; the
cover implied she was a poster girl for those of
us who were born to freak. Despite naysayers
and critics, she followed the strange and mystical
path that was placed before her. Intrigued by
this book cover and in search of inspiration, I
endeavored to learn more from her directly by
journeying to ask her spirit if I could merge with
it. I wanted to learn more about her life.

The drumming begins, and I set my intention.
Suddenly, I am standing in the back hall of a
church alongside Teresa. She agrees to merge

with me, and her body drifts into mine. My facial muscles become very tingly and contracted during the merging, as if my face is trying to rearrange itself to become Teresa's.

Wearing all white, I head down an old stone-floored hallway. I experience many things while in Teresa's body—the exhaustion of traveling in a horse-drawn carriage at night, moving from town to town. In the churches along the way, I kneel down in front of the altar and plead for Jesus to merge with me. As he does, I felt an intense ecstasy—pleasure almost to the point of pain. It is like being aroused at the level of the soul— an erotic, sensual, pleasure sensation—ecstasy. Afterward, I touch the sick or I fall down onto the floor of the church and allow people to touch me. As I move from church to church, the crowds grow larger.

I see great squalor and suffering, crying children, and very ill and dispirited-looking people who follow the carriage along the roads. I am exhausted but also in love with my work and my passionate connection to Christ. It is a miraculous marriage of sorts.

I feel a great joy in this merging and falling down and letting healing take place through my (her) body, which I get to know on a cellular level. I feel I can keep going, and I never feel alone. People speak ill of me, especially some of the powerful men of the Catholic Church. At night, when I sleep, my sweet surrender to this relationship of spirit with Christ is palpable.

Then the drum calls us back. This incredible experience is doubly strange as I have never felt a closeness with Jesus, despite being raised an Episcopalian. I don't have a distinct sense of who Jesus really was as an individual but instead feel the power of his spirit when I merge with him.

In the months that followed this encounter with Teresa, I enjoyed a deeper intimacy with my helping spirits. These sweet feelings settled on me at night as I lay in bed just before falling asleep. They were often stronger when I was particularly disheartened.

I found great pleasure in Teresa's exhausting life. I knew that I would never be a saint, but this generous experience showed me that living a life devoted to the spirits—Jesus in Teresa's case; Alice and others in mine—was a beautiful, deeply satisfying, and worthy life to lead.

Many other unexpected encounters with spirit followed this one. One of them was particularly unpleasant. But, by now, I'd become aware that even terrifying encounters, like mine with the black mamba, could have great significance. My job was to pay attention.

It wasn't just journeys alone that were teaching me. There were dreams as well. I awoke at 3:00

in the morning from one awful dream in which I was dying. It was vivid and gravely real. Metastatic melanoma had been found in several places in my body. I was lying in a hospital bed shrouded in layers and layers of gauze and blankets, with tubes all over me. I was barely recognizable.

In the dream, I was totally resigned to death. Charged with the responsibility to call my friends and tell them, I felt horribly overwhelmed. Worse yet, I had the feeling that I wasn't prepared to face the bardos of death—those intermediate states of consciousness between lives that the Buddha described—so that I could leave the earth. Great, I thought. I am dying, and I can't even get that right.

I understood, while in the dream, that there was one thing I had to do: *I had to love Mark without reservation.* I was also told (or more accurately, I heard) this warning: Anger causes disease. If I wanted to live a long life, to prevent this dream from becoming a reality, I had to love Mark in an unlimited way, and I had to meditate in order to prepare myself for death when it did come. The dream wasn't entirely horrible, however; in it, I was also able to feel the deep grief of my dear friends at the news that I was dying. I was more loved than I ever could have imagined.

When I woke up, I felt flooded with immense love and compassion for Mark. Just before going to bed the previous night, he'd been grousing about his sleep-apnea equipment. I was weary of him complaining about it. After the dream, I suddenly saw him in a completely new way. I was aghast at my response to his anguish. Tears sprang to my eyes and I looked over at him sleeping. I couldn't wait for him to wake up so I could tell him how much I loved him.

I crept quietly out of bed and headed into the living room down the hall to spend time writing out the dream. I immediately recognized that it was an awful lot like Ebeneezer Scrooge's dream in Dickens's *A Christmas Carol*. While it was uncomfortable thinking that I might be as bad off as Scrooge, I was grateful. I was being given a view of my own future, which might be dim unless I could "love Mark without reservation." As terrifying as the dream was, it was also clear to me that it was a gift from the spirits.

At 5:00 that morning, I heard Mark stirring to his alarm in the next room, and I immediately went to him and shared the dream and confessed: "I'm so sorry. I've been insensitive about your breathing. Please forgive me. I love you, and I'm going to love you in a better way." We hugged and tears streamed down my face. I felt Mark melting into my body, and there was an immense gentleness permeating the room, the house— the neighborhood. I was grateful for this literal wake-up call.

• • •

The more deeply I plunged into my work with the spirits, the more I realized that it was time to really let my medical career go. I sensed I needed some help with that, so I had a healing performed for me by a shamanic healer named Kris Thoeni. After the healing, she encouraged me to create a ceremony to empower my intention. To prepare, I carefully constructed a little coffin representing my career in medicine. I used an old cracker box as the base and strapped on an outdated hospital ID badge and a printout of several work-related emails—the kind I'd prefer never to see again. I covered it all in a tangled bit of black string that looked like a spider's web, to represent all the ways my medical career continued to entangle me.

I also spent some time thinking about the many gifts my medical career had given me—the privilege of doing years of challenging work that I loved, the gift of courage to trust my diagnostic skills, the fellowship of many brilliant and fun colleagues who were committed to doing great things for others, and (of course!) the sheer adventure of it all.

When I told him my plans for a ceremony, Mark sensed how important this process was for me and offered to join in. I was relieved to have a witness. Together, we opened sacred space in our backyard fire pit, as we had learned to do many workshops ago. I silently reviewed my intention to release my medical career fully, blew my intention into the cracker box, and placed the little coffin into the lively flames.

As the fire began to consume my cracker-box coffin, a very unexpected and miraculous thing happened. A beautiful ashen peony with a multitude of soft, fluttering petals bloomed up out of the blazing coffin's lid. Peonies are my favorite flower. They represent beauty, the ten-thousand-petalled nature of the soul, great abundance, and ease. Even Alice, my elephant guide, wears garlands of peonies around her neck. This ashen peony rising out of the flames was as strong a sign as I could imagine: *This new path will be blessed.*

As often happens when you do shamanic work with intention, a few weeks later, things literally start moving in "ordinary reality." The chief of my department at the hospital called to say that they were no longer sure they could continue to renew my hospital credentials unless I worked more frequently. I'd only worked a handful of days in the past two years. Momentarily, my ego wanted to protest. How dare they imply that my diagnostic skills could fade so quickly! But the part of me that was fighting was becoming quieter and quieter. He told me that he wanted to bring the issue up at the next staff meeting and asked if I wanted to be there for the discussion. I heard myself say to him, all calm and adultlike:

"I'm okay with whatever the group decides." And I really was.

After letting go in the fire ceremony, I suddenly recalled what my shamanic teacher, Alicia, a fierce and wonderfully made human, said about becoming a healer. She's a slender and powerful woman originally from Mexico, with fiery eyes and the loveliest way of expressing herself. "I hafff deeecided to coh-mmeeet my life to theeees work. Theees work *is* [pause] my [pause] life," she told us. She pursed her lips and raised her eyebrows as she looked out and into each of us and paused for a long time. In a way, it was a throw down. Alicia's words swirled in my head for weeks afterward and struck a chord deep inside me. Could *I* commit to this work for life?

I was putting everything I had into a new boat and leaving the known shore of medicine. This felt both charming and a bit sketchy, like Thor Heyerdahl's Kon-Tiki raft made of reeds—organic, soulful, and beautiful but perhaps not entirely seaworthy. I was seeking safe passage and a blessing—maybe even a miracle—to be able to serve as a healer.

Later that year, I took some time at the river near my house to do a second impromptu water ceremony on my own. I blew my intention into a small offering boat I'd made of wildflowers and birch bark and placed it into the current. With the slow-running summertime river, the singing birds, and the bees lazing in the thimbleberry blossoms as my witnesses, I silently made this commitment: I dedicate my life to doing this work. I commit myself to listening to the spirits and to being a conduit for help and healing.

All the confusion and dust around my life became a prayer to the spirits:

Make me useful.

Allow me to serve in the greatest capacity I can.

You know me.

Give me all I can handle.

Point the way.

CHAPTER 26

Into the Shadows

Every man casts a shadow. . . . This is his
grief. Let him turn which way he will, it
falls opposite to the sun; short at noon,
long at eve. Did you never see it?

Henry David Thoreau, *A Week on the
Concord and Merrimack Rivers*

Mark and I decided to attend an Explore
Your Shadow Self workshop. I knew that it
was critically important for a healer to be aware
of her own shadow as well as the dark side of
healing tools—sorcery. Not everybody out there
is working with the spirits to help and to heal.
The course had a shamanic basis, which intrigued
both of us, and I was anticipating that my shadow
self would contain hidden power which, if I
could find it, would make me a better and more
effective version of myself.

The workshop attracted some fifty participants
and took place in a rundown condo complex at a
ski resort. Our instructor was a warm, mustached
sort of Marlboro Man gone spiritual. He was in

his mid-fifties, sported a dark silk dress shirt and a bolo tie, and spoke often of giant, horrible, dark entities and all things shadowy. Most of his shamanic healing clients, he claimed, were "tough cases" referred to him by other healers for depossession work. He described how he often needed to do his healing work beneath large, door-sized mirrors to keep the entities he was trying to extract from "seeing" him while he worked. In all likelihood, he thought, if they "saw" him, they might come back to attack him.

While I didn't doubt our instructor's experience, to that point I hadn't encountered anything as awful as he described in my own (albeit limited) shamanic healing practice. Of course, it hadn't been all baby otters either. I'd danced with the fierce black mamba, and during one of my first intense shamanic experiences, I'd seen fleeting, unpleasant things with ghoulish gargoyle faces that looked vaguely holographic, like the ghosts on Disneyland's Haunted House ride. Some looked like spirits that I recognized as dead people with agonal expressions, but a few looked more diabolical.

One night during a powerful group healing, I had seen some ghoulish things go flying away as the client's healing took place. I immediately interpreted them as something that just did not belong—or, more accurately, as something that had to be removed in order for healing to occur.

When I asked other participants about them, they reminded me that there are entities in the Middle World that are not helpful and loving. They suggested that I ask my spirits for help. When I did, I was taken to a river in the spirit world and given a cleansing and protection. To my relief, the entities did not return.

This experience taught me that not everything shamanic is sweetness and light. Moreover, it showed me that help was there for me when I asked for it. I didn't have to face such things alone. And finally, I realized that acknowledging the darkness sometimes helps us come into the light.

During this shadow workshop, we were supposed to develop a method for feeling safe as we work shamanically. Marlboro Man's predisposition to speak of enormous dark presences wasn't helpful, however. He even invited us to consider putting a mirror under our own beds at home—just in case—to hide ourselves and "our light" from entities who might not have our best interests at heart. This just didn't resonate with me. The shamanic work I had done thus far was deeply soulful and touching. It always brought me a sense of deep peace. I wondered if perhaps I just wasn't advanced enough as a shamanic healer to encounter or recognize these enormous dark entities. I felt it was important to acknowledge darkness and its existence, but I wasn't feeling inspired to give it that much attention.

Midway through the workshop, we were sent on a shamanic journey to encounter our own shadows directly. I was relieved; I couldn't wait to meet mine. I lay down on the worn conference-room carpet, closed my eyes, tossed my wool challis scarf over my face, and let my body sink into the floor. I took a deep breath in and let out a heavy sigh, releasing accumulated tension from the day. The drumming began.

In my mind's eye, I headed down a path into the Lower World while simultaneously holding the intention to meet my shadow. And then I saw her—a life-sized plastic Dolly-Partonesque blow-up doll with huge boobs and creepy, overdone makeup. Unlike Dolly Parton herself, who is precious and sings like an angel, this image was off-putting, cringe-worthy. What I found most upsetting was that my distorted shadow had *two giant orifices*—her vagina and her mouth. My shadow was, very unexpectedly, a double-D, double-orificed, scary, clownish, *plastic,* bleached-blonde Dolly.

After returning from the Lower World, I sketched out what I'd just seen—the false eye-lashes, the boobs, the orifices—while shielding my notebook from my fellow participants. I didn't want them to become alarmed and call security. I was so confused. If this was my shadow, did that mean that I needed to apply false eyelashes and thick red lipstick to embrace my divine sexy, feminine power?

I protested to myself. Sexy, to me, is old-growth forests. It is deep, meaningful discussions with Mark, sacred *palo santo* incense burning in the background. Was the message that I should become a sex healer or therapist, as my mother once suggested when I was back in college? She seemed to think that, because I was so unabashed about most things, it might be a perfect career choice for me.

And yet, the boobs kind of rang a bell. From puberty on, I'd felt woefully inadequate. It didn't help that my breasts came in looking like swollen tubes—not at all what I'd expected after playing with Barbie dolls, seeing Brooke Shields in *Blue Lagoon*, or flipping through the *Playboy* magazines I found in houses where I babysat. There were so many things I didn't like about myself, and my boobs were certainly one of them.

At twenty-four, I decided that I could fix that particular short-coming with a simple, fairly innocuous surgery. At my surgical consultation, I dropped the paper gown as requested and the plastic surgeon took a good, long look at my now-exposed chest. He immediately gave me his clinical impression: "This is a mild tubular deformity that is amenable to surgical correction.

A lot can be done here, yes." That made me feel simultaneously worse—my boobs really *were* deformed—and better—there was a cure. I hesitated, wanting to be sure he really understood what I was saying: "So I'm thinking just a *wee* bit bigger—just to fill them out, you know?" He nodded, making notes in my chart.

Remember that I was on my way to becoming a doctor myself at this time, and could therefore rationalize that a legitimate medical problem like a wretched breast deformity simply needed correction. So my dream boob job became a much-needed medical intervention. I booked it and funded it with student loans. These new boobs were going to change me. *They would complete me.* I wasn't doing it to snag a man, either. I already had Mark. I was doing it for me, just like all the other happy women quoted on the plastic surgery websites. I was choosing mindfully to enhance myself.

Though Mark supported me in my decision, he was concerned about size, as I was. He didn't want me to look like Anna Nicole Smith any more than I did. When I woke up in post-op, the surgeon informed me in a hushed tone: "I had to make an intraoperative decision on the table to go a little bigger than what we'd talked about originally. I don't think you would have been pleased otherwise." I was too foggy to contemplate what this really meant.

While recovering from surgery in Mark's apartment, my formerly petite tubes ballooned into huge, shiny, tense cantaloupes. In the cramped bathroom, I pulled back the shower curtain as Mark brushed his teeth at the sink and his eyes grew large. He was unable to hide his reaction. I felt him retreating from me in mild horror, which was absolutely the opposite of what I'd wanted. I had thought boobs would make me feel more normal or acceptable. This was the first sign that it wasn't going to be so simple.

Finally, my new boobs settled down a bit, but they were still much bigger than I'd wanted—not enormous, but still too big for me. Now I was experiencing a whole new level of self-consciousness. I took to wearing baggy sweaters because I didn't want my astute medical school classmates to notice. I discovered that I wasn't cut out for this kind of exhibitionism. *Or was it honesty?* I found that, as my boobs got bigger, I shrank.

Several years after the surgery, I began to develop a complication often downplayed by surgeons when describing the procedure to prospective patients called "encapsulation." This occurs when a bit of scar tissue begins to envelop an implant and harden it. Now, not only did I want to hide my C-cups; I couldn't even lie on my stomach. Finally, I planned a quiet surgery out of town to reverse the original procedure.

After the surgery, my boobs slowly perked back up, restored to their small size—more Cate Blanchett than Dolly Parton.

At the end of the shadow workshop, we were put into small groups to do shamanic healings with each other. We sat in circles of six with the lights lowered. We each had an opportunity to be heard. When it was my turn, I shared my family history of bipolar disorder and depression. "My mom, my sister, my great-grandmother, and her mother all suffered from it," I said, "and sometimes it feels as if I'm not going to be able to escape. Does that make sense?" Heads bobbed in understanding. Then, a little hesitantly, I pulled out my sketch and spoke of my weird, blow-up-doll shadow. "I'm not sure what it means," I confessed. I hoped my group could help me shed light on it, but everyone just shrugged.

Finally, it was my turn to be healed. One by one, the others moved around me. I could hear rattles and whistling. Tears streamed down my face as I felt enveloped in love by these caring people and their helping spirits. Rumbling shifts seemed to be occurring in my abdomen. At one point, I felt as if I were being flooded with lightness—with pure ease. It was a wordless experience, as shamanic work often is. Later, they told me they had nullified ancient ancestral contracts and cleared out my psychic basement.

At one point during the healing, one of the kindly people working on me whispered loudly and clearly into my ear: "That shadow is not *you*, Sarah." I smiled through my tears. My chest heaved up in recognition of this sweet truth, and I let out a huge sigh.

CHAPTER 27

Hellbent on Honey

Not I, nor anyone else can travel that road
for you. You must travel it by yourself. It
is not far. It is within reach. Perhaps you
have been on it since you were born, and
did not know. Perhaps it is everywhere—
on water and land.

Walt Whitman, *Leaves of Grass*

The pilgrims planning to travel to India
were advised by the trip's organizers to
take an Ayurvedic herbal preparation called
chyawanprash. We were told it contained a
very high concentration of vitamin C (clinically
proven to boost immune function), as well as
other herbs and ingredients. I decided it was high
time to heed their advice and ordered it.

The chyawanprash came in a white plastic
jar about the size of a jar of peanut butter. I
unscrewed the cap and peered inside at the dark
brown, shiny sludge. I grabbed a spoon, and
reached in and retrieved (not without effort) a
very gooey mass of stringy, grainy, date-colored

stuff. I turned the jar around and stared at the ingredients. The list of herbs, plants, trees, barks, and flowers was staggering—mysore cardamom seed, bacopa leaf, ghee, sacred lotus flower, fig, true saffron stigma; the list went on and on.

According to the *Charaka Samhita*, a foundational Ayurvedic medicine text, however, chyawanprash is more than just vitamin C in a weird condiment format. It claims to prevent the flesh from becoming flabby. The ancient practice of Ayurveda, a Hindu-based practice of medicine considered alternative in the US, teaches that the three elements or *doshas*—*vatta* (wind), *pitha* (fire), and *kapha* (earth)—must be in balance in the body in order to enjoy optimal health. Chyawanprash is supposed to balance these three elements; it's essentially an Ayurvedic magic bullet.

I placed a generous spoonful onto my tongue. It was spicy, sweet, sour, and earthy—like an exotic raisin pulverized with the most unexpected combination of herbs and spices I had ever tasted. As I savored it, it felt like a wee bit of India getting inside me.

I drove across town for a potluck dinner with the small contingent of fellow pilgrims who also planned to travel to India. One of the women had invited us all to her home. Fat snowflakes floated steadily down in the dark, blurring the road's edges. Driving through the freeway tunnels along Lake Superior in the early winter twilight, I was suddenly overwhelmed with emotion. Snowfall like this has come to signify a blessing of beauty and love from heaven to me, the way rain is seen as auspicious in India. When you examine the flakes closely, each is an astounding unique work of fractal art. In my journeys, I have experienced the grace of merging with spirit and falling as a snowflake. We are constantly being showered with extraordinary blessings. Tears rolled down my cheeks as I felt waves of deep gratitude. *I'm finally going to India.*

I think about all of the suffering my family has faced in mental-health or spiritual crises of one kind or another. Sometimes it was hard to sort out what was my suffering and what belonged to them. It's my intention now to stay connected to my own soul's voice, while being loving and compassionate with all of them. It feels good to dedicate this journey to India to relieving this peculiar kind of suffering of the spirit.

The sweet gratitude I felt was quickly followed by waves of fear about what might happen when I was in India. Things that overwhelm me are sometimes made easier when I undertake them on behalf of others, so I decided then and there to dedicate my pilgrimage to those who suffered from depression, addiction, anxiety, bipolar disorder, and ADD.

When I arrived at the door, I was greeted by Catharine, our seventy-seven-year-old hostess, who was a slender lady with white hair in a pixie cut. She was warm and welcoming. On a tour of her home, she showed us her office where she does sand-play therapy with her clients. The shelves were stuffed with hundreds and hundreds of tiny figurines and objects to help people uncover the reasons for their own suffering.

We had taken our son George to a play therapist years ago when he was having tantrums in preschool, trying to figure out how to support him. I'll never forget when he showed me what he had created in the sandbox in one of the sessions—a black Jesus on a cross with an army figurine pointing a rifle directly at his chest. I was shocked at what was revealed by this simple exercise in play. It seemed obvious to me that he felt terribly persecuted. The therapist never offered an explanation, nor did George. Through the play therapy, however, the tantrums stopped, and he became calmer and happier. I immediately felt a deeper connection to Catharine after seeing her workspace. She was a healer.

There were eight of us present. Over dinner, I asked if the others were willing to share their intentions for going. Julia, a focused, former local juice bar owner, told us that she'd done the pilgrimage before, and she aimed to be of service to other pilgrims. "India is really, really a challenge for me," she told us. "It's exhausting, and I usually get sick, but it's also really amazing. I love it."

Catharine, who had recently been diagnosed with Parkinson's disease, said: "I'm really hoping to deepen my yoga practice. I'm only able to go with Julia's help," she added with a smile and a few tears.

Joy, a nurse, admitted that she didn't know exactly why she was going, except that she loved yoga and was curious. "If you love country music, you go to Nashville," she added with an impish smile. "And if you love yoga, you go to the Kumbh Mela."

The others weren't sure yet why they were going, but each, in his or her own way, felt called.

With the introductions out of the way, we exchanged notes on packing, three-pronged current adaptors, down sleeping bags, headlamps, and antibiotics. I was overjoyed to be sharing my anticipation with my new pilgrim friends.

I recognized that, despite the difference in our ages and the different reasons we felt we had been called, we were all willing to undertake what was sure to be a very challenging journey to be with sixty million people in India, so very far from Minnesota. Our collective apparent courage reminded me of one of my favorite Beasties in the South African bushveldt: the honey badger. This fearless creature doesn't bat an eye when diving into underground caves swarming with stinging bees. She's hellbent on honey.

PART THREE

India

Sometimes one must travel far to discover what is near.

Uri Shulevitz, *The Treasure*

CHAPTER 28

Agra

There is no way to prepare for the
mystical zap that is India. It's stunning,
tragic, hallucinatory, bejeweled,
smoky, overpowering.

Anne Lamott, *Some Assembly Required*

As dawn comes, the landscape is still cloaked
in dense, pure white, maddening fog, and
I'm able to catch only small glimpses of a tree
here or a vehicle there. I'm dying for visuals! I
need to know I'm really here!

After three hours on a bus, we finally take our
first break at a truck stop. I step off the bus into
night air that's smoky, mysterious, and soft. It's
incredibly welcoming—a lush embrace.

Day breaks as we enter Agra and the fog lifts
a tiny bit. The bus careens along at an alarming
speed. Where the fog thins, I catch glimpses—
families huddled around small fires at the road's
edge, scrawny dogs, and troops of monkeys
atop crumbling walls, as if sitting on bleachers
observing the show below. Despite India's

reputation for being the most spiritual place on the planet, with each new glimpse, I see that chaos reigns. These glimpses are like tiny sips of what I sense is the ocean of India. This is not the cinematic, charming *Best Exotic Marigold Hotel* India with colorful parasols, candlelight, and brightly painted rickshaws. This is gritty streetside India, where it seems that most are just getting by.

After breakfast, I grab my phone so I can take some pictures and jump onto one of the smaller buses bound for the Taj Mahal. In the parking lot, it is mildly chaotic, and our driver shoves away a one-legged child who's begging. My mind flashes to the film *Slumdog Millionaire*, my only reference for amputee beggar children in India. Often children are intentionally hobbled or maimed so they can become a source of income. It's distressing, and I feel momentarily helpless. But our guide is now motioning us to move along quickly.

As we enter the hushed side courtyard of the Taj Mahal grounds, I'm most struck by the number of wild birds within. Hundreds of squawking green parakeets flock from tree to tree, and small, white egret-like birds stand in stillness on the ground. Several different large kettles of hawks circle in rising spirals in the sky. Monkeys scramble up onto the high thick walls.

It's as if all the beautiful creatures also know that this place is sacred.

As sun pours in through the fog, an ethereal white light encircles everything. We pass through the inner gate and catch our first glimpse of the Taj in the distance. Wrapped in an embrace of glowing vapor, it rises regally from its broad foundation. Its silhouette is a perfect blend of feminine roundness and driving masculine spirit. The distant image appears to be almost transient; I blink to test its endurance. We hush and slow, as if stupefied by the beauty, before gradually becoming more aware of ourselves again. It truly baffles me how something this sublime could have risen out of the chaos lying just outside its gates. Then cameras and mobile devices are whipped out and people come alive again, wanting to capture photos and remember the moment.

From our vantage point at the gate, I spot many presumably well-to-do Indians posing for photos in brightly colored saris. Selfies are unself-consciously snapped. Indian teens cluster in typical urban get-ups—fitted jeans and neon T-shirts. There are a few preschool girls with large extended families decked out so opulently that it would make mothers on *Toddlers and Tiaras* want to pack up their makeup trunks and go home.

The kohl-rimmed eyes of infants blink back at me mythically. I've finally arrived.

· · ·

We continue on, past the grand reflecting pool, making our way closer to the main building. With our guide, we bypass enormous lines of presumably middle-class Indians wearing predominantly saris and dress shirts with slacks who are waiting to enter the main attraction, the mausoleum.

Small groups of four or five of us at a time are guided up a narrow staircase to the main entrance. We spill out onto a generous front terrace and walk slowly toward the grand arched entry, taking time to stop and examine the intricate flowers and vines painstakingly carved into the white marble exterior. There are fruits and flowers inlaid with yellow marble, jasper, and jade. I'm particularly excited to see the interior, as I have seen it several times in journeys, and I want to compare my Upper World Taj to the actual thing.

Once inside, I see a combination of geometric and more organic designs carved on the interior panels, similar to those my own journeys had revealed. As we tour the magnificent structure, I see that my interior world is now literally being made manifest in the external world.

Our guide leads us to the circular path around the tombs. The security guards seem to be truly enjoying their whistles, which hang on cords around their necks when they aren't blowing them. They seem to be channeling some kind of righteous fourth-grade gym-teacher karma by blowing on them constantly to keep us moving. But this is necessary, because we are all stunned into a trancelike state by the sheer scale and staggering beauty of the inner walls.

Despite being deafened by the screaming whistles and the intense crowding, I feel strangely calm and unafraid as we're herded like cattle through curved chutes into this sacred space. I feel as if I'm traveling through a living metaphor of the Buddhist wheel of suffering—*samsara*.

Samsara means continuous movement and the repeating cycle of death and rebirth in which we are trapped when we're attached to self, ego, and the external world. It arises out of a lack of awareness and induces suffering, fear, disappointment in life, and pain. I try to contemplate this, but it's difficult to be meditative while being thrust forward by bodies pressing against me and assaulted by constant shouts in Hindu punctuated by shrill whistles. I long to drink in all of this beauty in peace.

Finally, our *samsara* ends, and we're spat out into an anteroom where our Indian guide, a candid and warm man in his fifties who is dapperly dressed in business casual, shares something personal with us. It's quiet here, insulated from the hubbub, and we can actually hear him as he speaks.

"In the heyday of the Taj Mahal, this place was very much alive. Prayers were sung or spoken by musicians and singers twenty-four hours a day. It was a very charged and sacred atmosphere." For a moment, my brain transforms the entire place into a rad nocturnal Bohemian scene, with costumed revelers, incense sticks, candles, and live flute music. Pure theatre and magic.

"Today," our guide continues, "while music and live prayers are not routine, it is said that, between three and four in the morning, the angels still descend to the Taj to answer the prayers of the people. A few years back, during a time when my own family was experiencing very bad luck and poor finances and my brother had a brain tumor," he says, "my eldest son implored me and my wife to pray during this auspicious hour. We aren't religious people, you understand, but we wanted to honor his request. We didn't have much faith, but we wanted to help, so we were willing to try it.

"Every night, we set an alarm for three o'clock. When the alarm went off, we crawled out of bed and prayed on our knees. We asked for healing for my brother and for our lives to come back into balance. Within several weeks' time, my brother's luck had completely turned around. He made a full recovery and all of the family's relationships became more harmonious. We made a connection between this marked improvement and our prayers. Since then, we continue to pray at this auspicious hour, but now my wife and I don't even need to set an alarm. We wake automatically at three o'clock and get on our knees, praying for ourselves, our family, and the world."

Faith can only be gained through personal experience. I am suddenly aware that I'm here to pray that I can do what I'm being called to do.

After leaving the mausoleum, I join a few fellow female pilgrims and stroll through the grounds. A crowd of sari-clad Indian women gathers behind us as we walk along the wide gravel path, and I turn briefly to look back at them. They smile at me, and I smile back.

A few minutes later, one of the women fairly shouts to us, sharply, in perfect English: "What caste are you anyway?" Then they all begin to laugh. There's definitely an air of haughtiness to their laughter, and I'm caught off guard.

I look around at my group of Western pilgrims and imagine we must appear quite odd to the Indian women. We're sporting Danish clogs (okay, that's just me), bizarre interpretations of proper Indian dress—kurtas paired with black woolen long underwear (oh, wait, the underwear is just me again), malas, and hiker's backpacks. Even though we're trying to fit in, we're hard to categorize. I feel as if I'm back in my junior high locker room and the other eighth-grade girls are staring at my nakedness.

I try to dwell in curiosity and possibility, which

helps me feel connected and more peaceful again. Even though India is known for its spirituality, that doesn't mean that *bodhisattvas*, or enlightened beings motivated by great compassion, dwell on every corner. According to Tibetan Buddhism, a bodhisattva is someone who dwells in a sublime state. Those who are fallible, but worthy enough to attain bodhisattva status eventually, are said to be *arhat*. I muse darkly that there may also be another, not-so-sublime, state in which the noncompassionate dwell before they attain enlightenment—*asshat*.

After our visit to the Taj Mahal, we are taken by bus to a place where they make carpets. It's a hostage situation. We're held captive until somebody buys a rug.

We're given a demonstration of how the carpets are made. I hope for an early parole for good behavior, but, instead, we're taken upstairs and offered tea. I had forgotten how exciting this kind of captivity can be—the first time. I understand the allure and usefulness of beautiful carpets, but my view of things has shifted with our recent downsizing project. I'm trying to be more wary of acquiring things these days, and more interested in having experiences.

Most of the people in the room seem overjoyed, however, as if they've never been taken hostage before. They seem thrilled to be offered hot tea by their captors. I try to settle in and accept that this experience is also part of my pilgrimage. Finally, I ask where the restroom is and slip away alone to explore the second floor, where I discover a spectacularly embroidered, framed, velvet art piece depicting a pair of elephants mating. Grateful to find humorous relief, I fantasize briefly about mailing the piece to Mark with a note saying: "Wish you were here." Today, my spiritual side wins, and I leave without purchasing anything.

As our bus roars back to the hotel in the deepening twilight, I spot small groups of men and families huddled around small fires on the roadside and wonder whether they possess something we've lost—the primal, simple connection of being outdoors gathered around a hearth, not separated from one another by swaths of suburban, herbicide-treated lawns, or burdened by an endless abundance of possessions to catalog, store, return, sort, dust, exchange, or cart to Goodwill. What would life be like if each day began and ended around a small fire? Sharing a cup of chai. Telling stories. Just being with one another. Noticing the exquisite softness of the air we're breathing. That kind of connection is what I long for. By firelight, India seems essential, personal, and deeply interconnected.

CHAPTER 29

Mela-Mobile

India is not, as people keep calling it,
an underdeveloped country, but rather,
in the context of its history and cultural
heritage, a highly developed one in an
advanced state of decay.

Shashi Tharoor, *World Policy Journal*

O ne Sudoku-inclined pilgrim calculates our
Total Pilgrimage Bus Hours (TPBH) as
roughly forty hours. Some things are best left out
of the brochures. The first buses we board appear
quite modern from the outside. Inside there's
a groovy, cosmic paisley theme accented with
granny-inspired silky lingerie-like curtains.

As we ride in our far-out Mela-mobile,
time passes strangely. No *ayahuasca*, DMT,
drumming, or vision-inducing anything is needed
to put us into an altered state. I trade off between
staring out the window at India and striking up
conversations with the people around me. A lot
of the travelers seem to have a common bond
as devotees of the organization sponsoring our

trip. The crowd is predominantly over forty, with a few teens in tow with parents and a smaller contingent of twenty- and thirty-somethings.

Traveling days begin with a vague prediction of a four- to five-hour journey, which typically balloons into seven to ten hours. We bump along, accepting our fate. We watch pastoral India whiz by the windows, interrupted by the small, crowded cities we occasionally pass through.

Every few hours, the bus stops for a bathroom break. One hotel generously allows 150 of us to use their three (not all functioning) toilets. I cringe at the wreckage we leave in our wake. I begin to appreciate the charm of the more rustic roadside breaks where all 150 of us leap off to pee in the wild. The Sufi poet Rumi might have been talking about more than our infinite possibilities when he wrote: "Out beyond the world of ideas of wrongdoing and rightdoing, there is a field. I will meet you there."

The pandemonium of India's traffic—all the careening buses, overloaded trucks and semis, dogs, ox carts, pedestrians, and wandering cattle—reminds me of microscopic video footage of human red blood cells moving within a small blood vessel: flow occurs but not in a linear, logical way. It's as if each blood cell is in simultaneous, divine communication with the others. Some cells tumble forward at breakneck speed; others hold back and wait; still others creep along the edges for a while, only to burst forth when space opens up.

Traffic movement is similarly organic, as if India is one large organism, with the highways as her arteries and the rural roads as her capillaries. Witnessing the sights around me in this way, through a lens of blood-flow patterns, deepens my trust that there's a divine current running through everything that's orderly and peaceful. Our safe passage wouldn't even be plausible if there weren't.

When the sight out the front window is too much, I stare out the side windows at the world whizzing by. We're driving through rural Uttar Pradesh, a part of India that seems to have been forgotten. Some smaller towns look war-torn; so many ancient buildings appear to be bombed out and crumbling, but no cleanup crew has come to fix them. Some regions resemble the depleted, post-apocalyptic world that Dr. Seuss portrays in his book *The Lorax*, after all the truffula trees have been chopped down. Every square inch of nonfarmed land here is covered by some combination of drying clothes, dung piles, wandering animals, and people.

We pass through farmland, mustard fields of electric green and yellow that offer visual relief. I see many large, grand trees—many more *ancient* trees than you ever see in rural Iowa or on Wisconsin farmland. They're enormous and beautiful. It seems a wonder that these trees haven't been cut down out of desperation to make fires or to build things to sell.

Some trees have colorful flags posted nearby, in the same way that flags are posted at temples and other sacred places. When I ask a veteran pilgrim about this, she informs me that all trees are considered sacred here and that certain trees are prayed to for certain things. In Hinduism, each kind of tree has particular qualities and gifts it can bestow upon you if you ask—qualities like fertility, good luck, and health. *Everything that is, is alive.*

I begin to notice a peculiar pattern. Newer buildings have sprung up here and there that seem to have a modicum of hope built into them. These are single-story structures with towering projections of rebar protruding from their flat roofs toward the sky, ready to accept the bricks and mortar of a second (or even third) story, as if to say: I am only a beginning; we are not finished yet. A second story, maybe more, is on the way— maybe in the spring. Then again, maybe not. These buildings seem symbolic of the spirit that appears to infuse India's people. Despite the utter disarray and the cacophony of people and animals, there's no shortage of optimism. You can see this same anticipation in the smiles of the children; possibility is everywhere.

We observe as we go; but we are also being

observed. Our bus is a spectacle in the tiny towns along the Uttar Pradesh highway. Children rush toward our windows shouting gleefully, like girls I've seen running alongside a Taylor Swift tour bus. I'm perplexed; I've been to a lot of far-away places and have never been received like this. According to our in-country hosts, this section of bus-friendly highway was new this spring. Many local people have never seen a new bus like ours loaded with so many foreigners.

After seven hours or more, time passes excruciatingly slowly. It's late afternoon when one of our fellow pilgrims (definitely a front-of-the-bus person) begins to lead us enthusiastically in chanting aloud one of our *extremely long* assigned mantras. I recognize this irrepressible person because I, too, have been one. But now, I'm enjoying my moody Coldplay-induced trance state, watching the countryside out my window.

Mantras are syllables, words, or groups of words (often in Sanskrit) that, when repeated, have the effect of causing transformation. Pilgrims on both sides of the bus join our chanting leader, though it seems to me as if they do it more out of duty than out of passion. I remove my earbuds and, like a good pilgrim, try to chant the vaguely familiar words but discover that I'm feeling annoyed.

I fear this is the beginning of a larger problem

for me. Here I am, noncompliant student, on a sacred journey with a gang of seemingly devoted, mantra-chanting yoginis. What have I gotten myself into? Will they chant these unfamiliar Sanskrit phrases incessantly for the rest of the pilgrimage? Will I feel like a total spiritual heel, wishing I'd never signed up? Am I the only one?

Glancing around furtively between the seat backs, I notice other pilgrims half-heartedly phoning in their chanting or already returning to whispered conversation. The chanting quickly peters out. I'm relieved. I return to staring out the window peacefully and happily at rural India. I enjoy the pure solitude.

Ten or eleven hours into the bus ride, we turn off the highway onto a side road and proceed through a series of hamlets so small that our bus nearly scrapes the rooftop overhangs of the buildings on either side. It's almost like that last push out the birth canal—we just barely squeeze through.

Around 9:00 that night, we finally arrive at the land where we will stay for the Kumbh Mela, emptied of conversation and in the grip of full-blown jet lag. We receive a Downton Abbey–style welcome in the nearly pitch-black darkness from a team of smiling greeters standing all in a row sporting headlamps and waving at us exuberantly. Our safe arrival here is evidence enough of the sacred at work. Maybe it will be okay.

We step gingerly off the bus on stiff legs into the soft, cool darkness. Name badges are laid out on dimly lit card tables arranged in a grove of trees near the buses. We're instructed to go find our assigned huts, where we'll stay for the duration of the Kumbh Mela. Mine is number 39. In numerology, 39 reduces to 3 ($3 + 9 = 12$; $1 + 2 = 3$). Three, for me, is a divine number, as it's my life path in numerology. So even my hut is auspicious. I've only recently discovered numerology, the belief that a number can have a divine relationship with a coinciding event. At its essence, numerology is simply the idea that numbers are not random.

I was skeptical of numerology initially. How was it any different from magazine astrology or simple fortune-telling? Despite my doubts, however, everything I read about my life-path number (3) resonated with me. It said I was born to be creative, to express myself, to be the life of the party (at least sometimes), and to inspire others.

I had a dream recently in which I heard the words: "The number three is very important." When I awoke, the glowing digital clock beside my bed read 3:33. The numbers seemed to be hinting at me what path to take. For me, numerology is a heart logic. I've decided that, if something helps me, then maybe I don't need to have "proof" that it's true. *I just need to have evidence that it helps.*

I wander alone along the dimly lit paths to arrive at hut 39. Home sweet home? I prop open the thatched door and peek into absolute blackness. I can't see a thing; my mind leaps around, imagining what I'll see once I have light. I suddenly remember the headlamp in my backpack, switch it on, and pop it onto my head.

Leaning my illuminated head over the threshold, I discover that it's not terrifying at all. It's cozy. Four neat cots beckon, with mosquito netting hung above. Strapped to the center support pole is a light switch and an outlet for phones and cameras. The floor is covered in fresh emerald-green felt, like a positively regal golf course. This is the country club of hay huts.

My shoulders drop and I exhale as I swing my duffel up onto my cot to fish out my sleeping bag. I inhale the sweet fragrance of the warm, dry straw. The whole Bethlehem nativity scene makes a lot more sense to me now. I roll out my sleeping bag onto the cot and begin to organize my gear. This place is perfect for a new beginning.

Lights out. I lie in the soft embrace of my down sleeping bag and suddenly notice all the sounds of the Kumbh Mela. My cot is beneath our one, tiny hay-framed window, open now to bring in cool night air. I hear drumming and chanting alternating with what sounds like electronic dance music pulsing in a muted throbbing, yet powerful, way. I toss and turn as I listen. How far away is it? I can't tell. Where's the river from here? Arriving here in utter darkness is similar to arriving in Agra under a blanket of white fog. Once again, we've arrived somewhere new, but I can't yet confirm it with my eyes.

I know there are more pilgrims just upriver from where I am and wonder how many more. I send loving kindness to all my fellow pilgrims who've come from far and wide. I pray that we all find what we came to discover, that we're freed from suffering—and not trampled to death. Amen.

I love the pilgrimage schedule, because it mimics my own schedule at home—well, on good days, anyway. At 5:00 in the morning, I rise eagerly and get dressed by headlamp-light. I gather a few items in my backpack, bundle up for warmth, and walk to get a cup of chai in the main dining hut. Chai time is announced at 5:30 by a loud, clanging iron bell.

We were told at last night's brief orientation to honor silence until 8:30, unless there is a true emergency—in which case, whispering is permitted. I welcome this daily silence as a break from the near constant din of and interaction with the outer world.

Staying silent seems challenging for many of my fellow pilgrims, however. I assumed a bunch of yoga instructors and devotees of a meditational branch of yoga would relish a few hours spent in silence. A small handful of rebellious pilgrims appear to disregard the rule of silence completely, however, and speak in normal tones during morning chai. Others whisper to each other constantly, as if emergencies are everywhere. This morning, my "pain body," as Eckhart Tolle refers to our hypercritical unconscious, has a hair trigger and is casting its fluorescent glare on everyone.

Hot chai is a welcome source of heat after the chilly night. I place my empty metal tumbler into the plastic dish bucket and head out into the darkness. Wide gravel trails lit by compact fluorescent lights help me find my way to the meditation grove, which is surrounded by a low wall. There are perhaps a dozen huge old Banyan trees covered in leaves that create soft rippling waves of sound when they rustle. A few pairs of pilgrims' shoes wait at the entrance.

It's not completely silent outside either. People from far and wide seem to be waking up and getting their holy microphones warmed up for a chanting competition in which, apparently, the one who chants at the highest decibel level wins. The most amplified chant so far this morning is: "Svaha. Svaha. Svaha. Ommmmmm." (*Svaha* is pronounced "svahh-ha"). The sound of crackled chanting arrives in strange warped waves from upriver as well. Here in the grove, our relative silence feels sweet.

I take off my shoes, moving bulkily in my layers like a Sasquatch. It's around forty-five degrees Fahrenheit this morning. I've got on long underwear, a polar fleece jacket, a huge scarf, a wool hat, and a GoreTex parka. In my stocking feet, I enter the grove. The ground feels soft and almost bouncy, like cork. I learn later that it's cushioned with packed dung, an excellent and inexpensive insulator. We meditate on a bed of excrement. Put *that* in your metaphorical pipe and smoke it.

Like others before me, I pull a slightly scratchy wool blanket from the large metal trunk at the entrance of the meditation area and look around for a spot to sit. There's an elevated temple where some people are already sitting, but I don't feel drawn there, thinking it is intended only for advanced yoginis. Sitting near a tree seems like more fun.

Other pilgrims file in silently, claiming their spots. A few opt for the elevated, open-air temple housing the square *hoven* used for fire ceremonies. Others sit upright in plastic Walmart-esque chairs, wrapped in blankets.

The lights suddenly go out, and we're thrown into total darkness as the official meditation begins. I hear a musical tone from our campus loudspeaker and a low, beautiful male baritone voice begins chanting: "Ommm. Ommm. Ommm Shahnthhhhheeeeee. Shanteee." It's incredibly soothing. I'll hear many beautiful chants in the weeks ahead, but this simple chant is the one I enjoy most. I try to see who's singing, but it's too dark to tell, so I close my eyes.

Other Sanskrit prayers are sung, but I don't recognize them. The singer finally returns to the original melodious chant—"Ommm. Ommm. Ommm Shahnthhhhheeeeee. Shanteee"—and then falls silent. With an effortlessness I only experience in bits and pieces when I'm alone, I quickly drop into an easy meditation—unfocused focus—and time passes unnoticed. Even my pain body seems to nap in the presence of this sweet lullabye. A deeper awareness awakens and seems to be listening.

Slowly, the dawn chorus begins. The distant hum of drums grows as well, and the millions of chanting pilgrims upriver join the birds' refrain. Wind blows through the trees, gently dancing the fat, stiff leaves. I feel as if I'm listening to a muffled, underwater Wembley stadium full of prayers both beastly and human. Despite the clanging bells, rule-breaking pilgrims, and my irritable pain body, I have momentarily connected with the Om of it all. *This* is why I've come.

CHAPTER 30

Light Karmic Rinse

It is wonderful, the power of a faith
like that, that can make multitudes
upon multitudes of the old and weak
and the young and frail enter without
hesitation or complaint upon such
incredible journeys and endure the
resultant miseries without repining.
It is done in love, or it is done in fear;
I do not know which it is. No matter
what the impulse is, the act born of it is
beyond imagination, marvelous to our
kind of people, the cold whites.

Mark Twain, on attending the 1895
Kumbh Mela, in *Following the Equator*

For the Kumbh Mela, an enormous city pops
up out of nowhere every twelve years. And
it's been happening for *thousands* of years.
Every twelfth year, when the Ganges recedes in
October, dropping thirty feet to its lowest level,
this area goes through a population explosion.
Over the course of the Mela's fifty-five days,

fifty to seventy million people will pass through a seven-square-mile area. It's the largest gathering of humanity in recorded history. Roads are built, electrical wires strung on poles, toilets dug, and temporary pontoon bridges floated across the rivers—all to ease the flow of people and traffic, and to improve safety.

The Mela grounds straddle two rivers, the Ganges and Yamuna. The thousands of individual tents erected range from tattered canvas lean-tos the size of an apartment kitchen in Brooklyn to full-scale ashrams resembling airplane hangars at LAX. Each teacher or guru intending to share his or her teachings stakes out a spot.

On our first morning, after meditation, we're treated to a fascinating lecture on the origins of the Mela by Ben, the stocky, dark-haired, spiritual head of the organization hosting this trip. Gentle breezes cool us in the outdoor lecture hall as we sit on plastic lawn chairs. Ben's voice is low and soothing—perfect for inducing a nap. I try desperately to stay awake because his content is so engaging.

He draws a map of the Yamuna, Ganges, and Sarasvati rivers (the third being an unseen mystical river) that merge to become Ganga, as the Ganges is fondly called by all—arguably the most sacred river in the world. The confluence of these three rivers is known as the *sangam*, which is considered the most auspicious place to bathe. It's a power spot, where the veils between the material and spiritual worlds are believed to be thinnest and where oceans of karma can be washed away. Weirdly, it looks exactly like the place where I find Alice when I journey.

I stare at Ben's rough sketch on the drawing board. "All rivers are considered feminine," he tells us, "in the same way that we consider the earth to be feminine—our Mother." Suddenly, I see a penis-shaped (lingam-shaped) strip of land that seems to penetrate the crotch where the two feminine rivers (lady legs) come together, and I begin to see an obvious sexual metaphor of creation. *The sangam is the womb.* It's the spot where Alice always stands—an elephant in the womb. I glance quickly around the open-air, thatched-roof lecture hall, but no one else seems to be sharing this Bevis and Butthead "ah-ha" moment with me.

In the past two years, with Alice, I've received many mystical teachings about a river confluence where three sources converge to create a single river. In these experiences, I stand on a spit of land where the material and spiritual rivers (sources) come together. From this small patch of land, I observe matter and spirit merging with the third element—my mind, my thoughts, my consciousness—to form one beautiful, deep, powerful flow.

It suddenly hits me that this river is both within

me and without. As I returned to this spot over several visits, I eventually found myself sitting on this spit of land watching a single, wide, deep, powerful river, which sometimes had small candle offerings floating on it. The message seemed to be this: If I can create that state of peace in my own mind through concentration or focus on this little spit of land, I can be a part of bringing spirit and matter into form. I can, literally, be a part of the creation process.

Seeing my inner world reflected so literally in the external world stuns me.

Ben reports that, due to the enormous number of bathers, levels of *E. coli* bacteria in the river are extremely high, so we won't be bathing in the Ganges. Instead of taking a full dip, as pilgrims have done in previous Melas, we'll take a boat out into the sangam and sprinkle water over our own heads, saying our prayers there.

I can't believe my ears! No bathing in the river? I have mixed feelings about this announcement. That's why I'm here! Yes, I can dip metaphorically as well, but I hadn't envisioned this plot twist. I'm on a pilgrimage to bathe in the Ganges! How can I *not* bathe?

At the same time, I feel secretly comforted. I have an out. Maybe I won't need to discover how chicken I am to immerse myself in the river, to have my own faith tested. As I contemplate all these conflicting thoughts, I notice a truth arising in me. I've come too far to let fear stop me now.

Before salvation, lunch is served. After noshing on hot dal, fresh tangerines, and rice in the thatched dining hall, all 150 of us are herded down to Ganga and loaded into separate boats, all of them ancient and painted in vivid colors that are slightly faded by sun.

These boats aren't open on top like the boats I'm used to. They have raised, rough, splintery wooden decking on which we're instructed to perch. We're mostly middle-aged pilgrims, and, despite all the yoga *asanas* some of us have done, we're clumsy as we crawl and wobble into position.

Using their long steering poles, wiry boatmen move us quickly across the widest part of the river to the sandbar at the center. The current of the river quickly absorbs our little crafts and wants to take us along with her. Our boatman steps overboard into the strong thigh-high current and pulls us upstream with ropes that are secured to the other shore, digging his feet and legs into the wet sand to gain traction, his legs, arms, and torso visibly strained by his intensive physical labor. Though the current appears subtle on the soft rippling surface, Ganga's power is deceiving. It's going to be a fight to get to our upstream destination. I can only imagine what the Ganges must be like to reckon with when she's swollen to flood stage. Swallows dart and swoop in the sky above us, making shadows on the water.

As we slowly make headway and travel further upstream, we finally catch our first glimpse of the Mela proper—a rather vulgar, smoggy sea of neon-trimmed tents and flags. A great deal of dust has been kicked up by the millions of pilgrims, shrouding the whole affair in an enormous, hazy cloud. I'd conceived something utterly different—an event of great beauty. From this vantage point, however, the actual Mela resembles a carnival in an odd, oversized used-car lot in Kansas at the end of a hundred-year drought.

We soon arrive at the auspicious sangam, the powerful confluence within the river, though there's also a spot of land there. Here is where the veils between worlds are thin. This is the metaphorical womb (or the "holy hoo-hah," depending on your point of view) in Ben's sketch. This is the place where we will sprinkle our heads with water and say our prayers.

After spending eighteen months thinking about this moment of washing all my karma away and saying my prayers, I'm caught off guard. My boatmates and I glance around at each other quizzically. We all seem a little stunned. We don't call upon deities or invoke anything in particular as a group.

Struggling to keep our balance, we wordlessly take turns rather awkwardly leaning over the boat's splintered edge to cup a few ounces of river water in our hands to spill over our heads. I have a feeling of being in someone else's church—regimented and a bit silly. It feels like a fraudulent baptism. I try to say my silent prayers reverently anyway, and I feel a tiny, resistant voice growing in me, saying: "This is not *really* what I came here for."

After sprinkling ourselves, a more relaxed mood arises. We turn back downstream, floating with the current, taking in the sight of the vast, dusty assemblage of millions onshore. As we drift closer, I see small groups of men, women, and children bathing at the water's edge, taking their holy dips. They repeatedly bob completely under the water and back up, hands clasped at their hearts, eyes closed in reverence. We float right by a stunning bare-chested elder—a holy man, a *sadhu*—with a flowing white beard. Wearing nothing but a clean, white loincloth and a symbol of the sangam painted in white on his forehead, he stares at us in utter disbelief as we float by in our colorful boats. He seems as stunned to see us as we are to see him.

Another man sits in his riverboat parked on the shore in a meditative position—legs crossed, eyes closed. Out of habit, I lift my cell phone to capture the moment. Then, something inside me says: *Stop. Put your camera down.* I just observe him instead. I connect to myself and to this moment. This is the kind of beauty I'm seeking.

Thousands of yellow and orange marigolds—singly and in chains—float on the water and along the shoreline. They're gifts given to Ganga to honor her. They're offerings, or *puja*. She appears to take them in joyfully, surging in gratitude.

The next day, we begin the three-quarter-mile walk along the Ganges shore to the Mela entry gates, encountering other small bands of pilgrims as we go. The sadhus are dressed in marigold fabric, adorned with mala beads, and toting gleaming tin buckets to beg for their sustenance. When I catch their eyes, I see looks that are mostly serene. We nod at each other, smile, and say "Namaste," saluting the Divine in one another. We pass beneath a pair of towering telephone poles encased in digitally printed signage with messages of welcome in English and Hindi.

We enter at the fringe of the gathering. As we move inward, the crowds grow steadily. There's an enormous grid of temporary roads, complete with billboards plastered with faces of various enterprising gurus and "You are here" maps. There are waving neon flags, colorfully striped tents, and twinkling tinsel as far as the eye can see. Our large, unwieldy group of American pilgrims is a moving spectacle. The crowds here are mainly rural people who have never encountered Westerners before. Cell phones and satellite TV have not yet become ubiquitous here.

Whenever we stop, people gather to stare or to take photos. The looks we get run the gamut from stunned surprise to innocent curiosity, and a few who look mildly unfriendly or perhaps angry. The unfriendly stares remind me that I'm a foreigner here. I put my hands together in front of my heart, bow slightly, smile, and said "Namaste," which means "I bow to the divine in you" in Hindi. The unfriendly stares immediately melt into smiles and recognition. It's as if their wordless response is: "Ahhh, *now* I see you." They return my blessing, and I feel myself relax.

I see a sadhu with a noose around his neck. He appears to be hanging himself from a small post in an odd spiritual feat of self-strangulation. This is the circus aspect of mysticism—eccentric demonstrations by holy men of their superhuman capacity to endure diminished circulation or severe pain—walking on hot coals, being buried alive, or lying on a bed of nails. Vendors hawk mala beads, rice, Coca-Cola, and floral offerings. People move calmly along the dusty roads—women in saris, children, men on motorcycles, and camels carrying large loads.

Periodically, we witness a guru arriving in style.

Depending on the guru's status, he or she may arrive on a wagon covered in orange marigold garlands and satin banners, a low-budget version of a Rose Bowl parade float. Others favor the luxe approach. One guru arrived in his $80,000 BMW 7-Series, complete with motorcade and machine-gun-toting bodyguards. The ashrams also reflect the varying status of individual teachers. They range from tiny, makeshift tents to huge compounds complete with fountains, chandeliers, flat-screen monitors, and small shopping arcades.

I feel as if I've traveled to another realm, one where I don't know the rules or how to read the signs. I try to look back to find the path we've traveled, to lock onto a landmark, in case I become lost. I spot a nice, big temple on a hillside that fits the bill.

Our group pauses and breaks into smaller groups. I end up with a crew of about fifteen people, most of whom are new to me. We're all Americans—two couples and their tween- to teenaged children, a couple of fabulous single women in their late sixties, a few single men, and myself. I've met the older women before, and they're two of my favorites. They seem to carry a relaxed knowingness with them at all times. Their presence makes me feel safer and more solid.

We head directly for the sangam, the hot zone, the spot considered most auspicious for bathing. We'd seen it yesterday from our splintery boats on the river, but I'm a bit nervous about going there now, as I expect the crowds will be heavy. En route, we cross a pontoon bridge built to help people walk across the river in this nonmonsoon period.

Near the sangam, we see the acres of hay laid down to keep the river's edge intact for all of the bathers. There are crowds around fifty people deep calmly entering and exiting the river. The river's edge has been heavily sandbagged to preserve its integrity. The bathing area is punctuated by towering telephone poles with huge clusters of floodlights, which must illuminate the space at night. It has the feeling of a Super Bowl stadium—vast and designed for high-capacity crowds. Dust rises in a cloud that envelops everything. As we approach the riverbank, I see women carefully unwinding and rewinding wet saris, drying them on open sections of hay-covered ground. The colorful cloths stretch out like artful banners.

Though we're a small group, as we approach the bathing area, our presence attracts attention. Something in me wants to keep moving. First, two people stop to stare at us, then four, then sixteen, then forty—and now three army officials show up. I'm not sure if they're here to gawk as well, or if they're concerned that we're going to disturb the safe and pleasant flow of events.

Our small group's audience continues to grow. My Namaste strategy is only helping minimally. The army officials come closer. They stare at us. A vendor trots over and offers us the flower boats with candles that he's selling so we can make *puja*, sacred offerings, in the river. A few of my companions decide to buy. This draws in more people. Now we're surrounded by an even larger crowd. Some look friendly and some more stern. My hands are sweating, and I notice that I'm holding my breath. Beyond is a much larger throng of people and more are approaching.

I want to skip the *puja* boats and move on before this gets chaotic. My fellow pilgrims head down to the crowded water's edge to place their boats on the river. I gesture to a woman and her daughter who are already taking photos of us to indicate I'd like to take their photo, too. She nods and then proudly stands to pose with her daughter. We exchange Namastes and smile.

As we leave the sangam area, I look back. So much dust has been kicked up that I've lost track of my temple landmark on the hillside. I can't even see the temporarily constructed footbridge we just crossed to get here. It's all disappeared in a haze.

In the crowded lane leading to the Hanuman temple, dozens of vendors hawk rice, mala,

271

fruit, colored powders, and other basic supplies. A cow, bedecked with an orange satin cape trimmed in fringe and gold befitting a bovine superhero lingers in the shade of a large tree with her handler, who's collecting alms.

CHAPTER 31

Troubled

Peace. It does not mean to be in a place
where there is no noise, trouble, or hard
work. It means to be in the midst of those
things and still be calm in your heart.

Anonymous

The Reclining Hanuman Temple is auspicious because the monkey king it honors is in an unusual recumbent position. It's one of the most popular sacred destinations in all of Allahabad and known for being extremely crowded. Worshippers come to make offerings, or puja, and ask for a blessing or miracle.

As we approach the temple, I spot a small boy of about five dressed as the Hindu Goddess Kali, deity of death. Kali is the frightening form of the Divine Mother goddess. She accessorizes rather ferociously with decapitated heads for earrings and a string of human skulls for a necklace, and dwells near cremation grounds. Where worldly attachments are renounced, she points to the cycle of death and rebirth.

273

This small boy's face is powdered blue, his lips stained red, and he's wearing a long black wig and a white shirt shot through with gold thread. He's precariously positioned on the ground in the midst of this large crowd. A child-goddess-deity sitting in the street. The mother in me is worried that he will be trampled. I'm also aware he could be a slave for a gang of exploiters. I'm fascinated by this vision—the mythological costume, the contradiction. As we move along the congested lane, I notice a growing chaos. Army staff alternately shout and blow forcefully on their whistles. These shrill screams seem to be the only way to motivate the massive crowds to move along when visiting a holy site.

Our splinter group is led by a kind and relaxed twenty-something man who was raised in both the US and India. He speaks in Hindi with the Indian police at the temple's gate. The noise level is intense and the crowd is growing by the minute. There seems to be a certain pressure to get these foreign pilgrims into the temple while they still can. Our leader has to shout to be heard. Inside, beyond the dark threshold, a man with glowering eyes sits on a chair guarding an offering plate that has a few rupees and a single burning candle on it. I don't even remotely feel like giving this guy a Namaste.

We're instructed to slip off our shoes and put them on the sprawling heaps of footwear strewn near the gates. Our guide admonishes us that it's important to give alms for Hanuman when we are in the temple. I unzip the passport case under my top and get out a few bills to hold ready.

Several of us glance toward the piles of various footwear. Will we ever be able to find and retrieve our own later? My concern for my clogs is actually not all that petty, as they're the only shoes I brought with me. While removing them, I lose track of our group for a moment. So many people are moving through this space that it's disorienting. I spot my group and rejoin them. Apparently, *now* is a good time to enter the temple complex.

I begin to plunge forward as requested but get the sense that there's no turning back, so I hover and hesitate at the gate, feeling dread. Though I'm curious to see the inside of this temple, a deeper voice inside is shouting: "Stay out!" But if I refuse to go in, how will I ever reconnect with my group? I tentatively follow three people that I recognize.

The air feels heavy and dank, and, as I step in, I immediately regret my decision. Then the pushing begins. We're body against body, pressing on each other. A woman on my left and her tween daughter glare at me as they shove their way forward. I crane my neck to see if I can just go back to the place where I entered. My mouth is dry. My hands are shaking. There's no return, no way out—unless, of course, I shapeshift into a spider and crawl out on the ceiling.

As we are pressed forward, it becomes darker. The only light comes from narrow, high windows on the right side wall. These are lined with metal bars. My heart is hammering away in my chest. I scan ahead and see a central staircase descending into darkness. It's designed to support about three people, but a crush of four or five people at a time flows steadily downward. Nobody seems to return. We're going underground? *Too many fucking people in here.* I try to move to the right, against the flow of the crowd. More men, women, and small children push and press on me and glare.

I spot one of my fellow pilgrims about twenty feet away. I shout to him but, with all the whistles and the yelling, he doesn't hear me. My body surges into an adrenaline rush. I'm shaking all over now and unable to think calmly or logically. I close my eyes for a moment to call for Alice, perhaps in the same way that Gandhi reportedly called out to his own manifestation of God, Ram, as he was being shot. Immediately, I perceive her calm presence and I can *breathe* again. I'm reminded (yet again) that peace is always available, if I ask.

I remember that, in shamanic traditions, a frightening experience or dream can serve several purposes. It can spiritually "clear the pipes," by literally scaring the *hell* out of you so that you get more clarity and deal with whatever you need to for your own evolution, in the same way that an initiation or rite of passage can. But a frightening experience or dream can also be precognitive, serving as a warning to help you avoid danger.

I shout and wave my hands wildly, then put them up in the air and shrug to let an official-looking Indian man sitting on the half wall overlooking the dreaded basement know that I want out. "How do I get out of here?" I ask, enunciating in my clearest English. He points back toward the entrance. Then he shouts something in Hindi at me over the crowd and motions to the wall he's seated on. I'm confused at first, but then realize that he's asking me to give an offering by tossing it over the wall.

I remember the sweaty rupees I've been crushing in my hand and make my way over to him, flinging them over the wall. Presumably, I've tossed them into the basement, where everyone going down those awful stairs is headed.

I look back to see crowds crushing forward. I see no one familiar. I plead with the official again, asking as I point behind me: "Is that how I can get out?" He responds in Hindi, leaving me lost in frustration. *Think. No—don't think—feel. Alice is with me.*

I accept that I can't go back, so I stop resisting.

I turn and allow myself to be propelled forward, mentally clinging to this bit of Rumi's poetry: "Troubled? Stay with me, for I am not." Suddenly, without fanfare, I'm thrust (spat?) out into a crowded, but roomy, courtyard between buildings. It's flooded with sunlight! I'm suddenly free. I feel like kissing the ground. I made it. Thank you, God. Thank you, Alice.

On the road back through the Mela from Hanuman Temple, we cross a broad avenue where hundreds of sadhus are streaming back from a gathering of some kind. One arresting, bare-chested man is attired in particularly amazing accessories, with dozens of chains of walnut-sized mala beads and dreadlocks piled high on his head, which is topped with a towering white turban that brings his height to nearly seven feet. His chest ripples with taut muscles and his eyes shine. One of the men in our group stops him to ask if he can take a photo. I want to as well but feel a combination of shyness and a weird resolve to keep up with the group.

I get twenty feet or so ahead, then turn around wistfully, wishing I'd stopped after all. I see my fellow pilgrim in position to take the sadhu's photo. In the moment he depresses the shutter, the sadhu whips off the fabric covering his lower half, revealing his penis, which is sheathed gloriously in lush white and red flowers. The photographer is taken aback and abruptly lowers his camera. Ha! The sadhu is laughing and smiling broadly, like Alice in Wonderland's Cheshire Cat, as he slowly covers up his highly decorated bits and walks on. *Nothing is what you think it is.*

After returning to campus, I shower outdoors in one of the temporary closets kitted out with tiny electric light bulbs, using a plastic bucket and some precious heated water. It's a trick to keep my waiting clean clothes dry, as they are clipped to a clothesline inside the small enclosure. I begin to rinse away the dust and Eau du Kumbh Mela—a complex and heady mixture of musky human sweat overlayed with subtle notes of fried garbanzo bean snacks, dust, incense, and hay. This shower feels like a two-hundred-dollar hot-stone massage.

While I attempt to dress, I hear a couple enter the neighboring shower and begin to bathe together. I can easily hear their quiet sighs of delight as they embrace. It reminds me of how Mark and I used to do this when we had more time for such moments—lazy Saturdays in bed, showers. The years of child-rearing and long days at work have certainly taken their toll.

As I crawl into my sleeping bag around nine that night, the drumming upriver seems to heat up. "It seems to be getting louder and more intense,"

I remark to Julia, one of my hut roomies and a Mela veteran. She replies: "Oh, just wait until the tenth—it's electric!" February 10 is the most auspicious bathing day and will draw the largest crowds. There may be as many as thirty million people here that day. But despite our noisy camp and the swelling rumble of millions more people just upriver, there's a silence growing in me.

The rain begins sometime after midnight, and *enormous* buckets of water are dumped directly onto our hut's vulnerable hay roof. The roof begins to leak—slowly at first, in little spots, and then in little gushes. The wind whips the soaked saffron curtain against its hay frame, and sheets of heavy rain spray and soak the bottom half of my sleeping bag. These manmade quarters, so carefully constructed, are flimsy in the face of Nature's unlimited power

Then the intensity of the storm lets up just as quickly as it started, and we hear dozens of male staffers shouting to each other in Hindi and leaping around outside in the darkness, closing hay-shuttered windows and checking the integrity of structures.

It feels as if the intensity of the drumming called in the rain. I remember what the lady in white at our orientation in Duluth had said— that rain is auspicious, a blessing. I lie in my bed unable to get back to sleep. Half-soaked, my thoughts turn to the millions of exposed people living in lean-tos and tiny tents constructed of sheets of cardboard and plastic. Moms with brand-new babies. Tiny children. Thousands of stray dogs. How vulnerable they all are.

I've heard the crowds swelling upriver each night, and it's a bit scary. It also makes me feel a strange solidarity with all pilgrims, past and present. In a similar way, as my labor with our Josephine began, I'd felt an unusual unity with all women across the world and across time who'd gone through the experience of giving birth. I felt awed and afraid, but remembering those others before me helped me focus on my task of staying calm. It seemed that breathing was what spontaneously connected me to my earthly sisterhood.

We're now gathered at the bank of the Ganges in our varying states of vulnerability to pray and we've been purified, collectively, by this grand and surely auspicious rain. Our ablution complete, we are ready for ceremony.

CHAPTER 32

Kumbh Mela Redux

Live in the sunshine. Swim in the sea.
Drink in the wild air.

Ralph Waldo Emerson,
The Conduct of Life

Today I find a group of American women who are game to return to the Kumbh Mela. In our group, there is myself, a forty-five-year-old married mother of four and doctor on furlough, a retired teacher in her sixties, a forty-something mom from the corporate world, and a full-time grandmother, also in her sixties. As women, we've been advised to take a male along as an escort. Together we decide, perhaps naively, that it wouldn't be too reckless to go as an all-female team during daylight hours.

We're now forty-eight hours away from the royal bathing day, when the largest crowds are expected. I'm aware of previous stampedes, the worst occurring in 1954 that left 854 dead. With thirty million people on such a wee spit of land, anything could happen. I'm more than a little nervous about it, yet I'm unable to resist. There's still so much to see.

The dusty spiritual circus of colorful ashram tents, with flags and tinsel flapping in the breeze, sprawls endlessly as we head down the main dirt road on foot. I spot a colossal baobab tree that looks like a very stout and misshapen opera singer with dozens of skinny twisted and leafless arms outstretched to the sky. It's surrounded by sadhus adorned with mala beads. Someone in our group says it's the Ganesha tree. As I focus, I can see even from here that there's at least one obvious elephant head in the tree's bulging trunk. When I see it, I feel an electric zing of recognition in my body. I've got to get closer.

Ganesha is the elephant-headed God worshipped by Buddhists, Hindus, and others. Devotion to Ganesha extends far beyond India. He's known as the lord of new beginnings and remover of all obstacles. I leave the small lane, clamber quickly over a low fence, and head down a steep embankment and back up the hill to get closer to this magnificent tree. The rest of the group follows me. As I get closer, I plainly see numerous graceful elephant shapes in the tree's body—a curving trunk, a head with ears, a chest protruding. The bark is smooth and silvery grey, nearly the color and texture of a wild elephant's skin. The elephant shapes look as if they are sculpted from clay. The tree veritably shouts *elephant.*

A young Indian man sporting a red bandana has his forehead firmly planted onto the bark-covered brow of a larger elephant form and appears to be praying fervently to it. He's the embodiment of reverence. It reminds me that I also go directly to an elephant with my deepest pains. Alice is, in her own way, a slayer of life obstacles. Not wanting to interrupt, we give him wide berth as we wander around the tree, silently marveling at its massiveness, trying to count how many elephants we see within it. The tree's girth is akin to that of the giant redwoods in Muir Woods.

As we return to the front of the tree, an older sadhu impatiently pushes the reverent young man away from the main elephant form and motions to us with a smile, inviting us to come forward and experience the tree for ourselves. The Indian red carpet of spirituality is being rolled out for us yet again. It seems as if the only gracious thing to do is to approach. I hand my phone and backpack to one of my travelmates, sensing that I don't want to be burdened by them.

Mandapa is the Sanskrit word for "the laying down of the physical world," the lightening of our own burdens so that we can enter more fully into a divine connection. The word also refers to the area in an Indian temple where you remove your shoes and prepare to move into divine communion. It's the place where you leave ordinary life temporarily behind.

I lean my head down and go brow to brow—third eye to third eye—with this tree's main pachyderm. I sense a powerful and wonderful connection between us. My thoughts ask the tree to share its wisdom with me. I feel a strange sense of strength coming from the tree. How many hundreds of years has it been here? Perhaps even a thousand? How much suffering has it witnessed? I want to know so much, to have a deeper conversation with this wise and still friend. A few minutes pass, then suddenly I feel embarrassed, as if I'm taking too much of a celebrity's time at a book signing. It also suddenly feels too intimate.

We decide to return to camp via boat. My feet are grateful. We find an available boatman, clamber onto the familiar splintery deck, and head out on the glorious Ganges. Despite its intense pollution, Mother Ganga remains a regal jewel. The sinking sun and emerging twilight beautifully illuminate the riot of colors at the Mela.

The water's silky expanse reproduces the melon pink and peachy plum of the sky and the liquid gold of the still hovering sun. The boatman's silent paddling creates beautiful disruptions in the field of color-infused light. Together, we fall silent in wonder, as we move noiselessly along with the flow. Time slows as the blazing red-orange disc of the sun descends and a new palette appears—rose, baby blue, and tangerine meld seamlessly and ripple on the river's ever-changing face. It's eerily quiet despite the enormous buzzing hive of humanity nearby.

This ancient flow has provided water to three hundred million humans and other living things for thousands of years. The immense power of her current is palpable. She's terribly vital beneath, yet uncannily calm on her surface. If rivers are our Mother Earth's circulatory system, *in this place,* we're surely in her aorta, propelled by the force of her mighty heart.

After one of Ben's lectures, an announcement is made that formal mantra initiation is available to all pilgrims at the camp. Unexpected bonus! Despite my resistance to the longer mantras we were assigned, I wonder if a more personal one could help me.

Some mantras are quite specific—designed to heal snakebites, find husbands, or prompt conception. The land we're camping on here at the Mela was, I'm told, cleared of cobras with the use of mantras. Mantras have practical applications, but they're also used as incantations—words possessing the energy to create miracles or manifest desirable outcomes. The word sounds have a vibration. Seeking a mantra of my own, I head to Ben's office near the dining hall.

As one pilgrim is ushered out, I'm called into

a brightly lit space. Ben directs me to a cushion on the floor. As we get down to mantra business, a soft breeze suddenly passes into the room and briefly lifts the translucent white curtains.

I anxiously explain that I don't want to commit myself to a life in this particular spiritual tradition, but simply want to receive a mantra to deepen my meditation practice. He nods and smiles, then sets down his clipboard and lowers his head slightly to review the form I've filled out. He says he's curious about my path from physician to shamanic healer, asking with a smile and half chuckle: "Is there much of a demand for shamanic healing in Duluth?" I'm not sure if he's honestly curious or outright laughing at me, but I smile and answer:"There's a small demand locally, but I also work virtually by phone and Skype." "Ahhh," he replies and nods knowingly.

With a few simple words, Ben invokes protection of the space, as we do in shamanic practice, and asks me to be silent. I close my eyes. As I do, I drop very, very quickly into a state of meditation. Then something really unusual happens. Rather than the deep violet color I often see pulsating in my mind's eye while meditating, I see pulsations of many colors—purple, red, green—as if all my chakras are being scanned. Then I get the sense that Ben is dipping into some kind of sacred storehouse for a mantra for me. A few moments pass and then he chants the mantra he's bestowing on me—and it's beautiful to my ears. It feels so sweet and divine. I realize that it's not something I want to share with anyone else.

Ben takes a few minutes to explain the meaning of the sounds composing the mantra and how it ties into my life's work. The meaning of the Sanskrit syllables magically and elegantly expresses all I hope to do in my lifetime. It feels perfect. He instructs me, however, not to focus on the meaning of the words while meditating, that it's the vibration of the words that will transform me. "By repeating this mantra, something will begin to grow within you," he says. "It may grow into an oak, a lotus, or a peach tree. It remains to be seen." Mango would be nice, I think.

In the days that follow, I take my mantra with me to the sacred grove and something does begin to grow in me. I repeat the new mantra silently, using my mala beads in the way Ben had shown me to keep track of the number of times I repeated it. The mala keeps my hands occupied so I can focus on the syllables, in the same way that chewing gum helps me do my taxes and other less intoxicating chores.

I also notice myself chanting the mantra silently in my head after I crawl into bed. The syllables come to me spontaneously several times throughout the day. The mantra seems to keep part of my brain busy so my true self can connect with all that is.

As the sounds begin to nestle into my brain and body, I begin to trust their ability to grow something within me. Just thinking of my mantra brings me to a place of sweetness.

CHAPTER 33

The River

We can't help being thirsty, moving
toward the voice of water. Milk drinkers
draw close to the mother. Muslims,
Christians, Jews, Buddhists, Hindus,
shamans, everyone hears the intelligent
sound and moves with thirst to meet it.

Rumi, 13th-century Sufi poet

It's 5:00 in the morning on the big day, and I'm
feeling contemplative as I lie in the dark on
my cot. It's *Mauni Amavasya*—the New Moon
day on which both the sun and the moon are in
Capricorn—the day with the highest spiritual
power for bathing of the entire Kumbh Mela. My
sham baptism on the boat had felt insufficient. So
I'm hoping for a true baptism today.

The day before . . .

I nose around, asking other more daring and
reckless pilgrims if they plan to bathe. Surely
I'm not the only one wanting to do this. I keep
hitting dead ends. One of my fellow pilgrims
explains that the actual bathing is simply a

metaphor for the inner work we are doing here. Others are fearful about the pollution and the amount of bacteria in the river. I try to explain, in medical terms, that bathing in the Ganges is no more dangerous than changing a baby's diaper—assuming, of course, that you don't inadvertently swallow the diaper's contents. People stare at me blankly after I tell them this, as if I am one sandwich short of a picnic. I forget how trusted governmental recommendations have become.

Then I run into a vibrant, silver-maned yoga instructor who is on the staff. I tell her that I really want to bathe in the Ganges and that it is something I envisioned doing in community with others.

She agrees that it is beautiful to do it in a group and tells me that I may be able to connect with an Indian woman who has been bathing in the Ganges every day since we arrived. "I'll let her know that you'd like to join her, Sarah."

Thirty million pilgrims are expected on the grounds today. The sound outside intensified last night, overflowing and adding to the usual peak of drumming and chanting at 3:00 in the morning. A fresh intensity took over around 4:00, and now a new preponderance of flutes is rising over the enormous humming *Ommmm* of it all. I do an expedited loving-kindness meditation for all of the pilgrims. *May they be free from suffering. May I be free from suffering.*

I move quietly through the darkened hut to gather my backpack and head directly to the sacred grove, settling onto the dung floor with my freshly minted mantra and my rudraksha-seed mala. I fumble initially to move the beads as I've been instructed, with my right ring finger and thumb. As I settle in, the beads begin to flow nicely through my fingers. I'm feeling deep joy here, immersed in the beauty of the Ganges and the sounds of millions of chants and prayers from other pilgrims.

As my meditation comes to an end, I notice that several of the teachers are beginning to gather around the sacred fire *kund* in the grove. The fire leaps and crackles to life as it is prepared for our work today as a community. Offerings of tiny black mustard seeds, dried blossoms, and ghee are fed into the flames, which sizzle and pop as they're consumed. We'll be praying here later today to remove fear from humanity and to heal the earth.

The woman I'm supposed to meet for bathing today is nowhere in sight. I sit on a bench at the top of the stairs to the river. Fifteen minutes pass. I feel a bit panicky, as if this is my only chance. It's now thirty minutes past the designated time to meet, and I worry that they've already left to go to the river.

Finally, I spot an Indian-born American man from our group and ask him if he knows anything about this elderly woman who bathes. He nods and asks a nearby local staff member something in Hindi. The staff member gestures toward the main dining hut. The man from my group grabs my arm and says, "Come on!" his face lighting up, almost as if he's more excited about it than I am. I am swept along the trail. We're running.

We quickly find the older woman on the path near the dining hut. She's with a young man who assists her and her niece, who speaks English. The young man is dressed neatly in a vest and shirt similar to the ones our Ganges boatman wears. He's carrying a plastic shopping bag. Her niece has on a simple cotton sari and a cardigan sweater.

The man who swept me here explains, in Hindi, that I'd like to join them. She nods to me, unsmiling, and then seems to ignore me. Her eyes are dark and furtive. The niece is bubbly, smiling, and welcoming at first, but then her eyes drift to my outfit—long black yoga pants and a navy kurta—and she says, in a half whisper: "You aren't going to take off your clothes, are you? You can't, because it would be disrespectful." I quickly assure her I have no intention of stripping. I plan to immerse myself fully clothed. She appears relieved, then says: "Also, Auntie really doesn't like to talk at all during these things, so please understand." I immediately fall silent, happy to comply.

The four of us walk silently down the winding dirt road toward the village's path to the river. We pass through a grove of Banyan trees as the soft morning light cuts through the lingering fog in broad shafts. The onion-shaped dome of nearby Patanjali's temple peeks over the treetops. It's silent, except for the birds' sweet early morning conversations.

Auntie is petite—barely over five feet—and she walks in a slightly labored way with a stooped posture. She's focused and solemn as she moves steadily along the path. Her black hair is shot with silver and pulled into a neat bun at the nape of her neck. She wears a dark sari and a long, heavy cardigan to keep out the chill.

We come to the end of the road and pass through a large gate with a nod to the camp's guards, then take a sharp right and step down into an old, narrow cobbled lane with small bluffs on either side.

River-soaked local pilgrims returning from bathing stream steadily past us up the hill. I keep my head down, staying close to my group. When we arrive at the riverbank a few moments later, Auntie pauses and stands back, appearing to take inventory of the situation. The three of us wait for her direction.

The morning sun shines brilliantly on the river.

Several hundred local people are here in various states of bathing—some are in the water, others are already out and getting dressed. A few Indian army officers stand at the periphery, keeping an eye on things. I hear the shouts and cries of children. This place is alive and beautiful, vibrant with the flow of the river.

Auntie suddenly points off to the left and we begin to move carefully and silently along the shore toward her selected area. The young man spreads a plastic tarp on the muddy shore and indicates that we should all lay our dry things on it. I slip off my clogs and step onto the packed, wet silt in my stocking feet, not wanting to offend by setting foot on Auntie's possibly sacred tarp.

Now that I'm closer to the water, I can see hundreds of flowers, mostly gold-orange and mustard-yellow marigolds, floating and bobbing at the water's edge. Dozens of sticks of incense burn happily, having been poked into the river's soft bank.

I slip off my wool socks and step onto the cold, slippery ground. The riverbank is somewhat steep, making graceful navigation into the water challenging. Auntie removes her sandals and socks and, with the aid of her helper, steps gingerly into the river. She motions to me and to her niece to come closer and to cup our hands. I step into the river and stand a few feet away from Auntie.

Standing thigh-deep in the water in her sari, Auntie pours a few tiny, black mustard seeds into our outstretched hands and demonstrates how to moisten them slightly in the river and spread them on our faces. Her beautiful, warm, brown face, weathered by the sun, is now covered with the small black seeds. The niece and I both immediately do the same. I close my eyes and feel the sun warming us.

The water is brisk and refreshing, like the spring-fed Minnesota lakes where I'm used to swimming. After we've anointed ourselves with the seeds, Auntie begins to make her way into deeper water supported by her helper. My feet slip and slide on the slick, silt-carpeted river bottom. It feels as if I'm trying to balance on the curved surface of a wet clay pot that's just been formed. I slowly feel my way along the bottom into deeper water, encountering small, sharp pebbles along the way.

There are pilgrims all around us, but I feel a quietness within and without, as if the ordinary world has been temporarily snuffed out to lay bare this extraordinary one. I'm about mid-hip-deep in the water now and I gather my intention: *Please—I want to be of service in the world, to help others heal, to relieve suffering, or to do whatever it is I'm best suited to do. I want to become the highest possible mother, daughter, wife, and friend. This is my prayer.*

I plug my nose and make a series of three dips, being sure I completely submerge the top of my head each time. I'm relieved and so happy to have made it to this place, and so grateful that a way was opened for me to do this. My baptism is complete.

Or maybe not. Auntie motions to me. She pantomimes with her hands for me to go out into slightly deeper water. I'm confused. Do I require extra purification? She indicates that additional dunking is necessary, so I obediently move until the water is just above my waist. I repeat my dipping procedure, submerging my whole body and head three times. When I rise out of the water after the third dip, Auntie nods and her beautiful brown face breaks into a broad smile. She is pleased.

Auntie invites me to come closer again. She motions for us to reach into a plastic bag her helper has handed her that is filled with dozens of freshly picked flowers. I reach in and grasp a handful of soft, feathery, blossoms—deep-pink bougainvillea and mustard-colored marigolds. Auntie partially submerges the flowers cupped in her hand, then turns to the sun and holds the flowers up high, repeating the motions three times. Then she finally releases the flowers to bob downstream with the flow of the Ganges.

The morning sun is still fairly low in the sky above the trees flanking the river. As we make our silent offerings together, it seems as if we drop into slow motion. The sun seems to shine temporarily brighter and the river sparkles more vibrantly. The sun gives us heat, light, and energy without ever asking for anything from us. With our simple offering here at the river, we express our gratitude. We are all being held in the beating heart of this place—temporarily knit together by the sun, the silt, and the powerful moving water. Standing together, we are blessed—one body and one heart.

CHAPTER 34

The Grove and the Jungle

And one of the historical Buddha's
very first teachings, recorded in the
Avatamsaka Sutra, says "the Earth
expounds Dharma," meaning,
I think, that the very world we live in
describes how to awaken.

Jaimal Yogis, *Saltwater Buddha*

My fellow pilgrim Lloyd is a mystical-looking American with a flowing white beard and who sports a white kurta. He's a free spirit and appears to be completely at home here on the Ganges. When he tells me about himself, it's clear he's also a lifelong seeker. We get talking about shamanism, and he shares that his own mother's spirit appeared to him after her death to apologize to him for locking him in a psychiatric ward for two weeks decades earlier. His encounter with her spirit gave him a lot of peace. In retrospect, Lloyd says: "Being locked on that ward was perfect; it taught me to be compassionate." When he was discharged, he decided to become a psychologist. For decades, Lloyd had a successful therapy practice and loved his work.

Lloyd is curious about the shamanic healing work I do. "Would you be willing to do a healing for me?" he inquires, eyes hopeful. I laugh that an opportunity to serve as a healer shows up mere hours after my proper baptism in the Ganges. And it's not even lunchtime.

This is my first shamanic "house call." I'm used to doing healing work in my own sacred space at home or in a formal group setting, not in India on a riverbank. Over time, I've found my own way to open sacred space, a divine mash-up of several different methods I have learned. I beseech my healing spirits to help me out.

Lloyd and I agree to meet at 2:30 that afternoon down by the sacred grove. Lloyd is requesting a healing for his hip. He wants to be pain-free so he can do his work in the world as a "wandering bodhisattva," defined by some as an ordinary person who sets sail to be Buddha-like in the world, practicing compassion for all beings. His hip pain is limiting his mobility and his ability to travel comfortably.

The sun shines on us and a beautiful breeze blows through the large trees flanking the Ganges. We arrange ourselves on some borrowed wool blankets on the dry grass. I have only my rattle with me.

I call my helping spirits one by one as I move through the six directions (North, South, East, West, Above [Upper World], and Below [Lower World]. As I move through them, I feel each spirit I call arrive, and they place themselves around Lloyd. Then I lie down next to Lloyd and put in my ear buds so I can hear the rhythmic drumming that will carry me. I travel my own well-worn path up through the clouds and into the Upper World, a place filled with loving and compassionate spirits that are felt rather than seen. My spirits huddle close and give me a recommendation for a specific kind of healing. A unique design is given to me that I'm to bring back and "install" in Lloyd's spirit. But when the spirits give me the design, I feel suddenly embarrassed.

It looks like a lingam. It's a very simple primitive drawing that looks like a phallus—or I suppose it could be an open-ended cucumber or the broken half of a paper clip. But it feels phallic. I plead a little with the spirits, telling them that I feel embarrassed to give this symbol to a man I hardly know. What if he's insulted? The spirits laugh and then get serious with me. "This is the symbol," they tell me calmly. Firmly.

So, I return down the same path and bring the symbol back to Lloyd. I rattle in all directions to seal the deal, then return one last time to check back in with my spirits. Sometimes they give me a "last word," or something my client needs to know. I've discovered that these words are often very significant. This time, Alice instructs me: "Let Lloyd know his mother says she's very proud of him!" When I share the spirits' last words, I notice a tiny tear escape Lloyd's eye. Even if it appears that not much is going on, when feelings flow enough to bring a tear, that is often a sign that something is, in fact, happening.

Afterward, Lloyd seems quiet. I sense our special connection has come to an end.

Lloyd asks how he can pay me. I'm caught off guard. I tell him, since this is an odd circumstance, there's no need for him to pay me. But if he feels he needs to, he can pay me whatever he's inspired to give. I jokingly say that I'd be happy to receive a juice box at the next place we stop, as juice boxes seem hard to come by around here. He seems somewhat confused by this suggestion, but I'm just trying to be buoyant and leave things open to whatever he feels comfortable doing. I'm feeling unattached—at least to the money, if not to the outcome.

Next morning, 5:00 arrives earlier than it seems it should. Though it's hard to leave my soft cloud of a sleeping bag, I'm eager to return to the meditation grove one last time. Tomorrow, we depart for Khahurajo. The soft, cool darkness is dominated by the eerie cries of peacocks.

Everything sounds better, I think, when it's free. The peacocks are a mirror for how I feel—temporarily unfettered; not a mom or a wife or a daughter. I'm not expending energy to create a harmonious household. I'm not pulled in a million different directions. It's just me.

As I walk in the cool air, I feel submerged in sacredness. The peacock—consort to Quan Yin, the goddess of compassion—comes to mind again. Each of the eyes on this goddess's peacock's feathers represents her uncanny ability to "see" the suffering of humanity, to hear its cries for compassion. It's as if the mythology and animals of this place are designed to get us out of bed and guide us into seeing each other and caring for each other. "Wake up, wake up! There is suffering in the world. No time to waste."

The Kumbh Mela behind, we make the twelve-hour bus journey to our next destination. It's here I will finally meet Nathan, the man that everybody has been buzzing about with great rapture . . . their teacher! At our new camp in Khahurajo, I wake to the sounds of robotic chimes calling us to meditation. Dagnabbit, I've overslept. I quickly dress and emerge from our new hay hut.

The sun is just beginning to rise and subtle light begins to permeate the sky. We're surrounded on all sides by small, craggy hills studded with large, bare-branched trees. I see a few monkeys sitting as sentinels high up in the branches keeping watch over their troupe, just as I've seen them do in Africa. This camp is nestled in the jungle of India and looks an awful lot like the untamed bushveld I saw in South Africa—bare trees, cactuses, and dense thickets. There appears to be more irrigation here, however, because I've also seen bright green fields of mustard and many more large deciduous trees.

I trot off in the near darkness to the campus's brand-new temple, where I remove my shoes, go up the stairs, and enter the first inner chamber, my wool socks gliding on the polished granite floor. It's hot and airless in here. Eight others are already seated in silence in front of a beautifully framed pair of calligraphied yoga sutras. I sit and try to meditate, but I find the atmosphere extremely stifling—almost oppressive. After ten minutes, I leave, as catlike as possible, to try the next chamber.

This deeper chamber has a much lower ceiling. There are about twelve people meditating here. There is a large black-and-white photo of a swami on a low table. Under his penetrating stare, this room feels even more suffocating. I don't even stop to sit down.

The photo seems dark and leering here. I long for the soothing grove of trees on the Ganges and its soft, bouncy dung floor. I miss the river's sparkle and fog, her continuous movement. I feel stuck. I leave the temple to wander, seeking my happy place elsewhere, though today it seems hard to find.

Back outside in the early morning light, I finally settle under an old banyan tree and meditate. I'm seated on a small stone wall that has been built up around the tree's broad trunk. This tree is enormous and has giant, fat clusters of glossy leaves that provide lovely shade from the sun that's now fully risen. It's as if I am sitting beneath hundreds of lovely green umbrellas. I begin to notice the immense personality coming through the tree in the knots and gnarls of its trunk. I see a laughing walrus and an elephant seal. When I ask the tree what it has to teach me, it just laughs back at me.

After breakfast, we have our first *satsang*, Sanskrit for a gathering of like-minded individuals to discover the truth. Nathan, the spiritual leader and guru of the group, is to guide our gathering.

Before Nathan arrives to give the lecture, his assistant scrupulously clears every leaf and speck of lint from his elevated throne and the surrounding ground. Every single one . . . even those I can't see. This is clearly a devotional act and is performed with great reverence. I struggle with the idea of giving such reverential treatment to an individual (and not to the rest of the group). But I definitely feel this way about my own healing space, wanting the flowers on the altar to be fresh and everything meticulously clean and in its place to honor the spirits and clients with whom I work. I try to relax.

When Nathan arrives, I see a tall and slender man with a shock of white hair and large, dark, round eyes whose demeanor brings to mind a version of Kwan Yin, neither all feminine nor all masculine, the deity of compassion. He moves with care, as if he understands the importance of his role. He seats himself slowly in his elevated place, with his arms folded firmly across his chest. He takes a few minutes to look out smiling into the audience—a group of about a hundred of us. Before speaking, he sings a beautiful Sanskrit prayer. His singing voice is warm and soothing, the same one I heard over the speaker in the sacred grove on the Ganges. It must have been a recording. Nathan has been with us all along. He welcomes us and tells several stories in a heavy accent. One in particular captivates me.

"There is a cave here beneath the new temple, where ascended masters and spirits dwell as ghosts or discarnate spirits. You will each have the opportunity to make a visit to this cave if you wish while you are staying with us here in Khahurajo. This cave will only be opened at certain times, as we must give these soul ghosts periods of peace as well. It is their home."

Nathan goes on to talk about the new temple: "Some things take longer than others to mature or to accumulate wisdom. For example, elephants and stones have a much longer gestation period than humans. The new temple will take three years to mature spiritually, and only then will it begin to grow in its ability to light the flame of others."

So many people seem to be under the spell of Nathan. Most here are devotees who've known him for five, ten, or even twenty years. He seems like a kind and perhaps brilliant scholar; however, when he sits at the front of the tent giving his lecture, he crosses his arms tightly over his chest. It strikes me as odd that a guru would use this protective body language, this stance of self-defense.

Sam, a darling thirty-something, flush-cheeked investment banker from North Carolina and I compare notes on Nathan. After sitting through two *satsangs*, we both feel a bit confused by his teachings. Also, many stories are directed at his long-time followers—the punchlines seemed to be inside jokes of sorts. It's nice to know that I'm not alone. Sam shares his misgivings with me and confesses that he did some digging about the background of this group and discovered a few unsavory allegations.

The yoga establishment, like the Roman Catholic Church or any other powerful spiritual organization, has had more than its share of scandal and abuse. Sam adds that there are court cases with convictions of gurus for sexual misconduct resulting in mulitimillion dollar damages in the US. "I've got my reservations about the whole guru thing," he concludes. "Yikes," I say, nodding my head in agreement.

Hearing this reminds me how uncomfortable I feel, thus far, with this whole guru scene I'm witnessing. I was speaking with a devotee in the dining tent the previous night, when he shared, with giddy enthusiasm, how, during a period of deep confusion in his life, one of the organization's previous gurus had commanded him to immediately quit his job, pack up, and move across the country. They happened to be setting up a new ashram in the city the guru told him to relocate to. A recent documentary I'd seen on a yoga cult immediately came to mind.

Watching it left me feeling unhinged—and his story sounded not unlike the devotees in the film. These people, many of whom were brilliant and succcessful with families and marriages at the beginning, were depicted as extremely trusting and began to put their "leader" at the top of their personal hierarchy. Over time, the followers seemed to become more and more childlike: willing to do anything . . . sell their house, jettison their morals, and turn large portions of their income over to their guru in exchange for the priviledge of *belonging*. To be Loved. Saved.

When the jig was up, the members who remained were left isolated, deeply scarred, estranged from their families, and without financial security. To me, if you're a true spiritual guide, you wouldn't dare to tell anybody what they should do. You help that person connect with their own inner wisdom and empower them to make their own choices. That's, it seems, is precisely what yoga and all of the other great wisdom traditions in the world are trying to do—in their purest forms.

Sam and I also concur in our frustration over Nathan's apparent unwillingness to talk about the erotic symbolism on the Tantric temples here in Khahurajo. My local hired guide tells us that the temple figures are metaphors for the ways power or sacred energies move through the human body and spirit. That makes sense to me and resonates with the way deep spiritual practice—union with the Divine—can lead to feelings of ecstasy that are similar or identical to ecstatic sexual bliss. But aren't they also more than metaphors? Aren't they instructions as well? Initiations?

I know that when I've done certain practices—one in particular that I learned during the dancing-with-stones workshop that's not unlike yoga's Breath of Fire (*Agni-Prasana*)—I've experienced a kind of ecstasy that is different from, but closely related to, erotic pleasure—my "getting laid by the Universe" experiences . . . a kind of Dr.-Bronner's-peppermint-soap-on-your-undercarriage-all-over-body euphoria. These experiences weren't an everyday occurrence for me, but they were certainly part of my spiritual path.

With all the potential ecstasy to be experienced in spiritual practice, it's not surprising that, in every tradition—from Catholicism to Buddhism—there seems to be some trouble with sexual misconduct and abuse. Perhaps it's tempting to experience ecstasy on demand, rather than waiting for the Divine to gift us with it. As a February 2012 *New York Times* article by William J. Broad suggests, there are practices in the tradition of Tantric yoga that involve intimate acts.

> Hatha originated as a way to speed the Tantric agenda. It used poses, deep breathing, and stimulating acts—including intercourse—to hasten rapturous bliss. In time, Tantra and Hatha developed bad reputations. The main charge was that practitioners indulged in sexual debauchery under the pretext of spirituality.

Having a close friendship with a passionate owner of several yoga studios, I know how infuriating it is to her, and her community, when prominent figures blatantly and unscrupulously use their power and position to gain intimate access to vulnerable women. I wonder what Tantric practices we're *not* going to learn about during our brief pilgrimage. Sex for the purpose of enlightenment? With the spell that some devotees seem to be under, it seems there would be nothing they would not agree to do for their teacher. I know, too, that the path I have chosen isn't immune to abuse; just as there are unethical gurus, rabbis, clergy, there are also unethical shamans.

Sitting on folding chairs in the sun, I share with another fellow pilgrim, a long-time follower of Nathan, that I'm struggling to find meaning in his lectures and that I find much of what he's saying confusing. She smiles beatifically and says: "His kind of storytelling is different; he's able to 'read' the room. He's able to see right into all of our minds and souls and give whoever's there exactly what they need."

I feel as if she's being a bit condescending, as if I'm too dense to get what's going on, even though Nathan may be giving me what he "knows" I need. Then again, I wonder if this is a case of me needing to become more humble so I can learn something new. This is either a whole new way to see Nathan's lectures, or it's the most brainwashed perspective I've ever considered buying into. Sometimes the measure of a good teaching is how much it irritates you or helps you discover your own truth. I'm definitely irritated, but I have yet to discover the pearl of wisdom being cultivated.

The next day, I try to listen with new ears and apply the idea that a deeper teaching may be happening here, one that's aimed right at me. But I find I'm even more challenged. Nathan is, inexplicably, *all smiles* as he talks about the recent tragic incidents at the Mela, the deaths and reported drownings. Just before we left Allahabad, we learned that my fear of a stampede was not so farfetched. Tragically, thirty-six people were killed on an overcrowded train platform, and there were rumors of a pontoon bridge collapsing and some of those on it drowning. Nathan's smiling seems incongruous. He makes a joke about the dead bodies floating down the river and laughs about how their families will probably say that it's auspicious or fortunate that they died in such a holy place during the Kumbh Mela.

Perhaps I am confused, but Nathan seems to be mocking the pure, childlike devotion that some pilgrims bring to the Mela—their belief that bathing in the river can solve all their troubles, the idea that God is a benevolent, paternalistic force. His attitude seems to imply that the pilgrims' extraordinary faith in God is somehow laughable. What's wrong with trying to reframe a loved one's death as a gift? Or trying to understand the terrible things that happen as part of a divine order? Or going bathing in a river with hopes that it can change everything? Or praying for a miracle? Maybe Nathan's laughter stings because I bathed in the sacred river just days ago, asking for my own miracle.

I understand that we must take responsibility for our own actions and lives, but I find the kind of reverence the pilgrims have so touching. Several of us nondevotees discuss afterward how strange and even disturbing what he is saying seems to us.

One day, Nathan spends a lot of time in a lecture pointing out that everything is not as it seems. He says research has shown that many "holy" sadhus are illiterate, not the learned men many perceive them to be. He says a large number of them have criminal records. He says: "The nearer to the lamp, the darker it is." He seems to be calling out the truth about holy men everywhere. I think about the allegations Sam mentioned and I wonder, is there something I'm supposed to be worried about here?

This is not to say that Nathan doesn't teach *anything* that resonates with me. He does. For example, he says: "If you want to know if your spiritual practice is effective, ask yourself how comfortable you are in your own skin. Ask how joyful you are inside. Ask how much space you create in your own heart." I wholeheartedly agree with this. And for rituals to be meaningful, Nathan says, we must put our whole selves into them. Paying a priest to do a ceremony for you is easy, but if you transform your kitchen, your living room, and your bedroom into a temple, that's much more powerful. Everything can become *puja*, an offering to the Divine. Your home. Your actions. Your relationships. Your whole life. Amen.

CHAPTER 35

Temples in the Rain

Every act of rebellion expresses a
nostalgia for innocence and
an appeal to the essence of being.

Albert Camus, *The Rebel*

It begins to rain. It rains hard, on and off, for days. This isn't supposed to be the rainy season, and we're wholly unprepared. Several of the huts flood; nearly every roof leaks; duffle-bag contents and spirits are dampened. I'm so frustrated today about the lack of silence in the main tent before sunrise that I'm a complete crankypants. It's as if everyone has forgotten why we're here—to engage in spiritual practice. *Damn it.* I hide at a table at the back of the dining room, drinking chai and silently simmering into my journal.

To make matters even worse, a well-intended fellow pilgrim pulls me aside to tell me that I'm "too pretty to walk hunched over" and then tries to correct my posture on the spot! Yikes! I know she means well, but it feels like a critique of my very being. Don't tell me I have pesto in my teeth. Not today. And please allow me to be Quasimodo for just this one week, especially since it's raining in the jungle and everything's become a muddy quagmire.

After several days of relentless rain, even the main dining hut roof begins to leak. There's not a dry table or chair left. With nowhere to escape the damp and cold, our spirits are diminished. Today, we're scheduled to visit a temple several dozen miles from here, Jata Shankar, but it's not clear whether the roads are even passable.

At breakfast, Nathan announces that we have two options for the day. We can either take our previously planned day trip (his face glum and serious) or we can stay put and visit the cave (Laughing Buddha smile and eyes twinkling). He then explains that a stone down in the sacred cave beneath the new temple is suddenly giving *darshan*, meaning that the Divine is manifesting somehow in the stone. By simply viewing it, we may possibly become enlightened or receive a teaching. Just how long this underground darshan has been happening is unclear.

At this moment, I have little interest in darshan. If it's happening here, can't I see it later? I'm dying for an adventure, even in the pouring rain. I need to get out of here. Everyone else seems to be shimmying with excitement at the idea of a basement darshan. Then Nathan says: "After hearing your options, does *anybody* still want an adventure? Please raise your hand." No one else seems to give a downward dog about going on a fresh adventure.

Half-crazed by rain and a feeling of suffocation, I boldly raise my hand, flinching reflexively from the glares I expect to receive. A few other hands shoot up. Not many, but I'm glad that I'm not alone. As I glance around, I note that the hand-raisers are fun people—Sam, Jo Anne and her son Jon, and a few others I've yet to meet who appear smiley and lively. Lord have mercy.

It's decided that, instead of sending the originally scheduled three buses on the temple adventure, they'll send only one for those of us in need of excitement. Or is it escape? I'm thrilled. I feel as if I can't stay here for one more yogic minute. Our group of roughly twenty adventurers gets completely drenched running down the flooded driveway out to the bus.

On the bus, we discover that it's still raining—inside. The roof of the bus leaks steadily. But the leaking roof scarcely dims our joy. We're free! We come up with an inspired and some-what uncouth way of staying dry. It involves ferociously chewing lots of gum and then using it to tack torn garbage bags to the bus ceiling to create a makeshift tarp. It works for a while, but then water collects in pools on top of the garbage bags and periodically baptizes us. We finally give up and just get wet.

While riding, we sing a hodgepodge of tunes: kirtans, ancient call-and-response Hindu chants embedded with healing mantras that have now been made popular in the US by Deva Premal and others; the Flintstones theme song; Bob Marley and John Denver favorites. Our spirits are most definitely Rocky Mountain high, despite the dampness. When we arrive at the Jata Shankar temple grounds, the rain suddenly stops. Surely, this is an auspicious day.

We stop at the foot of the hill in the touristy market to purchase offerings of sugar, coconut, and grains. Just as shamans make offerings to their beloved spirits in thanks, or when they ask for help, Hindus offer gifts in a sacred exchange with their deities.

The Jata Shankar temple is perched at the top of a long, winding staircase on which we encounter wandering cows, scampering monkeys, and a few other pilgrims. This is one of the most charming and beautiful temples I've seen. It's covered in mythical murals painted in a vivid, childlike palette that are reminiscent of Sunday paintings—the primitive and winsome amateur artwork you can find at estate sales.

The inner temple contains a complex riot of wacky and wonderful devotional offerings that pilgrims have placed on the altar, including flowers, foil balloons, children's toys, and other gifts. Sam and I take turns offering the sweets we purchased and saying prayers on our knees in the temple doorway, which is being attended by a young priest clothed in effortless sacred chic—a simple shirt and a cloth wrapped around his lower half, a fantastic headscarf, and minimal, yet effective, jewelry.

After we leave the temple, Sam whispers conspiratorially in my ear that he finds the priest incredibly sexy. I inspect the long-haired young priest with new eyes and understand. There's often something alluring and powerful about people we see as having access to the spirits. I smile back at Sam.

We board the bus again, where we wash down our lunch of naan stuffed with dal with mango juice from little boxes. We return to campus damp but happy.

The sun finally appears again and things begin to dry out. Today is our last day to visit Khahurajo. Alone, I wander and ogle the amazing temples here at the Unesco World Heritage site one last time. The temples are spread over a broad green lawn dotted with enormous ancient trees. Each building is covered in figures, the most striking of which depict humans engaged in all sorts of erotic activity, from simple breast fondling to large outright group-fornication scenes where *everybody* is in on the action—in any way they can be. There are penetrating headstands and other gymnastics—even bestiality.

The figures and faces are broad and curved, evoking a sensation of softness. Bliss and ecstasy are palpable on the faces and in the positioning of the bodies. Everybody is really having a good time here. It's as pure a depiction of ecstasy and interconnectedness as I can imagine. Did someone model for these pictures and was it considered an outrageous activity at the time? Or are they simply an artful celebration of pleasure? Or was it, in fact, Tantric instruction for sacred transformation. Perhaps these figures depict the nectar of immortality—the idea that, in divine connection, we can taste a little bit of that grand sweetness.

Maybe it's because I only have a few days left, and I'm starting to feel as if India is slipping away from me. Maybe it's the wadded-up rupees burning a hole in the passport case that I've worn around my neck since the first day. In either case, my old desire to take my adventure home with me returns. I'm hungry for souvenirs, and I need to make a clean kill. And as someone once said: Nothing haunts us like the things we didn't buy.

I wander through a few of the shops, stopping to admire an antique cast-brass figure of the Hindu Lakshmi, whose face has already been adoringly touched so many times by the devout previous owner that her features have been worn away, rendering her faceless. Like the Creator. God. The Universe. This is the kind of devotion I seek to experience. I want to be so faithful and devout that I wear away layer after layer of suffering through prayer with only my repeated soft touch. This is the kind of faith that can create miracles. Enamored of this figure, I inquire, but learn that it is, in fact, an antique and well beyond the limits of my budget.

I have a modest shopping accident at a government-sanctioned gift shop. I tell myself that means that fair trade is guaranteed. I purchase my very own cloud-like pashmina (it's an investment!), a beautiful embroidered silk coat (I'm *quite sure* I can wear it, "Iris Apfel-style," into my nineties), cotton sari fabric, a brass Ganesha, and bathrobes for my mom and my sister. I'm trusting that it's okay to acquire a few more beautiful things.

On our last evening in the jungle near Khahurajo, I fortuitously stumble into a second chance to visit the underground cave that contains the stone that reveals the divine. A small group of people are hanging around the main building waiting for Nathan. I'm intrigued, yet unclear about why I want to go. I guess I'm simply curious. What is this *darshan* like, I wonder. How does this spirit reveal itself? Will I be able to perceive it?

It seems that another divine opportunity has been placed before me. And my going seems sort of predestined, as I discover the group of about a dozen just as they're about to leave.

A few long-time devotees chat casually with Nathan as we all begin moving toward the temple. I keep my distance. In this final opportunity, I don't feel any draw to make any more intimate contact with him. It's about 8:00 in the evening, and the sky is dark and riddled with bright stars. We follow the dimly lit path to reach the temple and silently remove our shoes before we walk up the slippery polished stairs and into the first chamber, the *mandaba*, where we symbolically lay down our worldliness and prepare to open to the sacred. Then we descend halfway down the staircase leading to the underground chamber and line up. This subterranean part of the temple is even darker. My eyes are trying to adjust, straining to see through the dimness. In a soft whisper, we're told by one of the staff to wait until we're called in by twos or threes.

It's a very murky but swanky cave, with a polished granite floor and minimal lighting. I shift silently back and forth on my feet as we wait for the first group to finish. I am a wee bit excited to see what the stone is all about.

My turn arrives. My mind feels oddly blank as I casually step across the threshold and into the cave that's lit almost imperceptibly. We are slowly led to a spot on the floor where we are instructed in a whisper to sit.

When I look at the stone perched there in the center of the room, I immediately see it—or rather, *him*. It's not pleasant. A colorless hologram leaps out at me—the gaunt face of an old man. His facial muscles stand out in sharp relief and he has an intense, penetrating stare. It's nothing new for me to see a face in a stone—I often see faces in trees and stones—but this is different.

The face feels terribly unfriendly and seems to be looking right at me. *Through me.* It is clear and fully detailed. Photographic. It's similar to the ghost-like faces I used to see until my spirits gave me a protection to prevent it. Instead of being agonal or suffering, however, it seems very intent on something. I'm not sure of its intention, but it is disturbing.

As this goes through my head, Nathan slowly walks over to point out the vision on the stone with his finger, in case we've missed it. Then he returns to stand directly behind where I'm seated on the floor. I stare uncomfortably for a few moments at the face emerging from the stone, then I notice the presence of Nathan immediately behind me. I can feel his legs just inches from my back. Suddenly my brain is flooded with memories: The giddy guy who moved across the country on command, Nathan's ominous commment, "The nearer to the lamp the darker it is," and the ridiculously scrupulous cleaning of Nathan's throne by his dedicated attendant. This sudden total recall along with this disturbing holographic face converges into a forboding inky wave.

Something in me wants to flee. Something here is wrong. I have an overwhelming feeling that I need to get out of here right now. It comes in a loud whisper from within my chest, from my own soul. I sense that this place, this darkness, is dangerous for me. I quickly disengage from the penetrating stare of the unpleasant gaunt face in the stone and, as quietly and composedly as I can, rise and leave. Momentarily, I wonder if I'm leaving too soon in anyone else's opinion, but I don't care. I've simply got to go. The other two pilgrims who entered the cave with me seem to take my exit as a signal that it's time to go, and we all walk out together. We silently slip our shoes back on in the darkness and leave separately.

As I wander back to my room under the bright stars, I reflect. I sensed a lot of power in that face. And it did not seem to want me there. Or rather, I did not want to be there with it. Perhaps the spirit dwelling in the cave wanted nothing to do with me. I suspect that he may be an ancestral type of spirit, the kind that's truly only interested in helping his own devotees, his own "family."

According to shamans, these ghosts and disembodied spirits of the Middle World can have a very human and flawed nature, as their compassion is selective—unlike spirits dwelling in the Upper or Lower worlds. Some ancestral ghosts choose to remain here in the earthly realm to help only those to whom they're devoted—family members and other loved ones—and those who are devoted to them. They haven't evolved enough to have love and compassion for all.

With sudden clarity, I see that *I don't need the spiritual clutter of another guru or another tradition.* I didn't come to India to seek a guru or another religion or tradition to follow. I already have a connection to my own helping spirits. While lying in my bed in the darkness with my headlamp on, I page back through my journal and discover my notes from Nathan's lecture earlier on: *It's imperative to enter a cave inhabited by spirits with reverence. This is where these ghosts rest. It's their home. Not all soul ghosts are compatible with us.* Perhaps my mere curiosity wasn't well received. Perhaps having a clear intention before entering would have changed my whole experience. Whatever the case, this much is clear: For me, this spirit is most definitely *incompatible.*

I'm truly trusting my inner guidance now, and it feels good. I also have a clear understanding that this cave and this tradition are not for me. But neither do I feel a need to dismiss this experience of darshan. I felt a real sense of power there in the cave, and I don't need to judge it. That spirit may indeed be a valuable teacher for others. Maybe this is why I've come all this way—to recognize that what I already have is perfect and beautiful; to learn to trust my own path.

Despite this uncomfortable experience, I realize how grateful I am that I came here—and to those who made this miraculous adventure possible. Without it, I would have never met Auntie, or bathed in the Ganges, or received my mantra initiation from Ben, which has truly helped me take my meditation to a deeper, sweeter place.

I rest in sweet silence. I feel newly unshakeable and possessed of everything I need to step forward.

PART FOUR

Return Home

There is nothing sweeter in this sad world than the sound of someone you love calling your name.

Kate DiCamillo, *The Tale of Despereaux*

CHAPTER 36

The Way Back

The ache for home lives in all of us.
The safe place where we can go as we are
and not be questioned.

Maya Angelou, *All God's Children
Need Traveling Shoes*

The return trip to Agra is grueling and bumpy. We take a completely different route from the way we came. For hours, we drive through what can only be described as an open field, but one with exercise-ball-sized potholes. We bounce along, occasionally passing over bridges with flimsy guardrails that look like Popsicle sticks. For perhaps forty miles, there's no recognizable road because the two-lane highway simply vanishes before us.

We stop for lunch and laze in the sun in a fancy-ish hotel courtyard overlooking a river with house-sized boulders in it. I feed some of my leftovers to the most forlorn stray dog I've seen yet. He gratefully and politely gobbles it all up. With this tiny offering, I feel as if maybe, in this homestretch, I have relieved a small piece of the suffering in India.

After staying in hay huts by the Ganges, the hotel in Agra feels like the Four Seasons. I can hardly contain my excitement and head to my room for some luxurious time alone and a nice, hot shower that doesn't involve damp clothes, and muddy feet. I'm aware now that I only need a bucket of water to do the job, and I shower quickly, wanting to use only what I need. I'm grateful for the bounty.

In the morning, I drag my belongings to the porter's desk and order my first pot of black coffee in twenty days. I relish every single drop. As we mill around waiting to board the final bus to the Delhi airport, Lloyd, the white-bearded psychologist for whom I did the healing, approaches me. He presses some folded bills into my hand, looks me directly in the eyes, and says: "Thank you. Since our session on the Ganges, my hip has been nearly pain free." We smile and hug. I'm delighted.

After thirty-six hours on buses and planes, I land in Duluth. Mark picks me up at the airport accompanied by Katherine, Josephine, Charlie, and Spirit Frances the Wonder Dog, who leaps irrepressibly into my lap for the ride home. George is off with friends. Everyone seems to have a sweet glow of happiness—an aura of love—around them.

"Mom," says Josephine. "You are not going to believe it when you see our rooms!"

When I ask what she did, she answers, "Oh, you'll see!" with a huge grin.

"It's going to be really nice to have you home," Mark tells me.

"Are you admitting that I am slightly indispensible, Mark Seidelmann?" I tease. Then I relent and tell them all how good it is to be back home and how much I missed them all. Charlie is more pragmatic, asking immediately if I brought anything back for them. I tell him I have a few things for each of them, and he shouts with glee. In fact, everybody seems to be fairly bursting with joy! These are my people! We hug and hug and hug.

At home, I'm immediately ushered off to Katherine's and Josephine's rooms, which have been rearranged and restyled. Charlie then grabs my arm and proudly introduces me to his new hermit crab. "His name is Mr. Krabs, and I'm taking care of him all by myself," he tells me excitedly. For once, it is on Mark's watch and not mine that the family menagerie grows.

As I walk through the house reacquainting myself with this familiar space, I marvel at how wonderful everything looks. The countertops are clutter-free and glowing. The fridge is stocked. Nobody seems to have been kicked out of school or met with any other disaster. "The kids helped,"

Mark reports. He looks fine. In fact, if anything, he looks more relaxed and content than I've seen him in a while.

After we eat a beautiful welcome-home cake made (with party sprinkles!) by Josephine and Katherine, I hand out the special stone mala beads I selected for each one of them—grounding black onyx for Charlie, heart-centered rose quartz for Josephine, turquoise for Katherine (it's her favorite color), tiger's eye for George (who's partial to big cats), and rudraksha seed for Mark. They seem genuinely thrilled. The kids move toward their rooms to squirrel away their sacred new treasures.

The depth of my blessedness settles on me like a soft, well-tattered quilt. *This is my temple.* Leaving all of it for a little while has taught me an enormous lesson: Despite all of my fretting, *it was just fine for me to go.* And while I was learning something deeper off in India, it seems that my whole family was learning as well.

I want to broadcast this on a megaphone to every mother or person who feels tied down by their circumstances or otherwise reluctant to leave their post for an adventure: "Go! Seize your adventures! Everyone will benefit!" I'm excited and ready to return to my sacred work here as mom, partner, lover, writer, and healer.

Everything I do is an offering. Everything is *puja.* Everything is prayer.

Even sweeter yet, in the weeks that follow, I notice more harmony between Mark and myself. It seems that we've found an easier way to co-exist, while still retaining our own uniqueness. Maybe we're just more grateful. He's looser, letting me be me. He's not constantly trying to clean up behind me as I turn the kitchen into a temporary disaster every time I cook. And I find myself intentionally being a bit neater. Maybe we're both just being more conscious. Mark smiles mischievously and tells me that something has changed in me—that I'm easier to be around. Apparently, there's also more honesty between us.

A month later, while visiting my sister Maria in Los Angeles (who is now happily thriving!), I discover some kooky monster drawings at the Hollywood flea market. They're colorful, freaky, and made out of vintage book pages. I buy several and, at home, frame them by replacing my diplomas and Board certifications with the drawings. This shift makes me so happy. The diplomas tell of my accomplishments, but they no longer reflect who I am. I lean the newly framed drawings on the fireplace mantel—a place of honor.

Then, I have a somewhat scary dream about a brown recluse spider dropping from a dead branch onto me as I lay on the couch. Ackkkkk!

I wake up just after it crawls into my sweater, and I freak out. It is so vivid that I know I need to investigate more.

Curious, I re-enter the dream via shamanic journey and discover that, despite its menacing reputation, this brown recluse spider is a new spirit guide stepping forward to help me with my writing, to help me weave a web out of my pilgrimage and other stories from my life. Her name? "You can call me Charlotte." On the journey, she shows me that she spins rather unusual webs. I immediately recall one of my favorite quotes from E. B. White's *Charlotte's Web*: "It is not often that someone comes along who is a true friend and a good writer. Charlotte was both." When I return from the journey, I immediately Google "brown recluse spider"—knowing nothing about them except the awful medical complications of their bites—to learn more. I discover that these spiders actually do spin unusual webs—*a disorderly thread creates its lair*. This feels so completely apropos for me that I can hardly believe it. After that, I reread *Charlotte's Web* and go on to read collections of E. B. White's essays and an autobiography, which I find deeply inspiring.

The pesky web that had entangled me in my old career as a physician was being transformed into a new kind of disorderly, yet helpful, design that I can weave as I continue to walk my path as a writer and a shamanic healer.

A few months after India, I return to northern California to the Foundation for Shamanic Studies to attend a program. We spend most of the days preparing for an important initiation ceremony scheduled for the end of the week. The mood is somber, to say the least, and one person elects not to participate.

I stand in the group that is singing together in the near dark. As the singing continues, I experience overwhelming emotion and tears come. My voice wobbles. My body begins shaking all over, and I feel so much—what it is, exactly, I cannot say. Fear? Joy? Surrender? Or perhaps all three becoming one?

Suddenly, I am falling and land curled on the cushioned floor on my left side in a fetal position. I immediately plunge into what I can only describe as an all encompassing and riveting embrace of love and extraordinary compassion and I hear the words: *I am here.* I immediately understand this to mean God. Then I hear: *I am with you always. I am with you on each step of your path. I am in everything. I am everywhere.* I feel simultaneously that I am being held and that a giant hand is reaching for mine—the hand of God. The Creator. The Universe.

I experience an instantaneous understanding of

and connection to the painting of God touching Adam's finger on the Sistine Chapel ceiling—something I had seen with my own eyes but never understood before. I am overcome with joy and sobbing with gratitude. *I can see so clearly now.* My mind's eye floods with throbbing, all-encompassing purple light.

I am in the overwhelming, paralyzing presence of God—or rather, I choose not to move, afraid that it will somehow disconnect me. I am held in his vast outstretched hand. I begin to see flashes of past experiences and to understand on a very deep level that each relationship in my life—with Mark, my mother and father, George, Katherine, Josephine, Charlie, Maria, even Suzi—has been perfectly orchestrated by this powerful force.

In a moment of intense wonder, I ask this presence: *"Are you Alice?"* The answer comes back: *I am Alice. I am in everything, everywhere, in each step you take. Do not be afraid. Do what your heart desires. I'll make a way for you.* I understand that I have nothing to fear and can create whatever I desire, knowing that I am supported.

The embrace I am in is so sweet, so immensely tender, and so loving that I don't want it to end. I am marinating in intense light and love, soaking it in. Then, I notice that a few of the others in the room are slowly beginning to sit up and leave the circle as we had been instructed to do earlier in the evening. Part of me doesn't want to awaken from this dream. But I am still fully aware of the room outside my inner experience. My teacher's voice reverberates inside me, reminding me that there is a discipline to this work.

My head is completely congested from crying by now. Slowly, slowly, I uncurl and sit up, preparing to leave the room. I am taken by the hand into the night air in silence by a fellow healer and rejoin the other initiates in a quiet room. I feel like an infant must feel after a warm bath and feeding, ready for sleep and resting sweetly in its mother's arms—the snuggly, drunk-on-milk peace that passeth all understanding. Eventually, as the minutes pass, I realize that this experience isn't transitory; it is in me, and I can leave it and return to it. I return all of my consciousness to the small room.

I later journey to ask Alice what happened to me that night. She tells me that my heart was opened and filled with compassion. I was also integrating the belief that there is great love for me here and that the spirits are constantly conspiring on my behalf. She tells me that this heart-opening happened so that I can go forward without any fear.

Since this profound experience, I have felt much less fear about my path. Someone said recently that we are the "great forgetters." I rise each morning to *remember* with my practices and meditation, and sometimes I still forget. Fear still creeps in and, when it does, I am almost embarrassed for forgetting that I am loved. *No matter what.*

This experience lingers like a subtle fragrance. I feel the presence of God, the Universe, the spirit more strongly now, especially when I am alone at night before bed. As I lie curled up on my left side, a strong memory of that comforting embrace emerges, and it soothes me. I now feel an intimacy with the Great Spirit that I had already experienced with my helping spirits. I am also aware of my own soul in a much more powerful way. I feel and see and know this beautiful lotus inside my chest, and it sometimes illuminates when I need to be reminded to reconnect with myself.

This is the single most beautiful, joyful, and significant experience of my entire life, *thus far.* I've been rendered calmer and more sure of my connection to the Divine than ever. And this is good, because more things are starting to happen.

CHAPTER 37

Mollie

Toward calm and shady places I am
walking on the Earth.

Anishinabe (Ojibway) song

In late summer, I receive an email from a local man named Cleo. When I call him to respond as he requested, he tells me that he found my name on the FSS website. "My wife, Mollie, is very sick," he told me. "She has cancer, and she's really wanting a shaman to come. She's at the Hospice House. Can you come?" His voice sounds calm, but I detect a note of urgency. I tell him I can be with her the next morning and ask if that works for him. He says it does.

Just before I hang up, something prompts me to say: "And Cleo, if something happens and you need to call me tonight, just call. I can get over there, okay?" He gratefully accepts the offer.

I wake up the next morning and get dressed, making an extra-special effort to look nice. I put on white jeans, a bright blue Indian block-print top, and red shoes. I want to honor this work and this family. I check and double-check my bag to make sure that my sacred things are all there—incense, earphones, the MP3 player with the drumming audio file, cloth for making an altar, a candle, my rattle, and a cloth to cover my eyes.

I arrive a few minutes early and sit in my car, warmed by the autumn sun. I've come full circle. Now, when faced with a dying person, I feel capable; I know I have something to offer. I know how to become a bridge between this world and the spirit world. This is not to say that I know what's going to happen or that the healing will be successful; but I know how to help in this very specific way.

I enter a sunny, beautiful room that faces into the woods and meet Cleo, Mollie, and one of their daughters, Katari. Cleo's kind brown eyes dart around anxiously, like a shepherd on watch. Mollie has been helped out of bed and into a wheelchair.

Mollie and I clasp hands and look at each other. I introduce myself and explain how, together, we can do the work that she's requesting. Her eyes are alive—alive in a way the eyes of those who've forgotten about death are not. She understands how she and I are going to proceed. I step out of the room with Cleo for a moment to ask the nurses at the desk to help us create privacy for the healing.

Out in the hallway, Cleo tells me quietly, but

with urgency and amazement: "Right now—I mean this morning—this is the most awake and lucid I've seen her in weeks."

I nod and smile at him gently: "Her soul is ready to do this work." I learn that Mollie's mother was deeply connected to the Anishinabe (Ojibwe) Native American tradition and had taught Mollie many things as a girl about living in the world through that tradition.

When we return to the room, I look at Mollie. "Let's begin by you telling me what it is you want to ask from the spirits. With what would you like help?" In this moment, I suddenly realize that I have no idea what she may be asking for.

"I feel as if there are parts of me that are missing somehow." Mollie looks at me, her eyes searching to see if I understand.

I repeat back for clarity: "There are parts of you missing, and you'd like them restored?"

"Yes," she responds, closing her eyes tightly for a moment and then opening them again, satisfied that I understand her request.

I tell her that I will begin by calling my helping spirits. "You'll just hear me rattling. Then I'll put in my earbuds so I can listen to the drum while I ask my helping spirits what kind of healing they recommend. Then I'll let you know what that is and you can decide if it's something you want to proceed with, okay?" She nods.

We draw the curtains to create as much

darkness as possible, then I light the candle. Cleo and Katari are sitting at the edge of the room; I stand next to Mollie's wheelchair. I've laid my kantha quilt made of women's saris down to journey on. Using my rattle, I begin to call my loving, compassionate spirits from the six directions. I feel them, one by one, gathering in the room. I feel as if every prior event in my life has contributed to the unfolding of this precise moment.

The sound of the drum helps carry me to the Upper World, where my spirit helpers gather around me and give their counsel. I return and report back to Mollie that they recommend a soul retrieval, and ask her if she wants to go ahead. She nods her willingness.

In the shamanic view of the world, soul loss can happen for many reasons. In fact, many indigenous shamans believe that it is the most significant cause of illness today. When we are conceived, our souls are complete; imagine them as golden balls of pure light. Over time, different things happen to us that can result in soul loss—trauma, fear, assault, verbal abuse, surgery, accidents. Even experiences that may seem "minor"—being teased, being shamed by a teacher—can cause pieces of the soul to splinter off.

Soul loss can also be the result of "soul stealing." Or perhaps that is too harsh a term.

For example, a mother, out of love, holds onto a part of her son's soul when he leaves for college because it's too painful to let him go. Or a partner holds onto a piece of a lover and then dies, still holding onto a part of their soul. A shaman may have to travel to the Upper or Lower World to fetch that fragment after death. And sometimes, you give a part of your soul to another (out of love) or surrender a part of it out of fear. However the soul parts are lost, shamanic practitioners can return them with the aid of their helping spirits.

Soul power enables us to journey effectively in our lives—to do what we came here to do. Without sufficient soul power, we are vulnerable to being influenced by suffering spirits and to negative energies consciously or unconsciously sent to harm us. This can lead to physical illness as well as depression, anxiety, and other forms of mental illness. That's why this healing work is so important.

Alice and I fly over the landscape in the Middle World (the earthly realm) to search for Mollie's missing soul parts. Because the soul is so exquisite, the spirits often use beautiful objects to symbolize its different aspects. The first of Mollie's soul parts appears as a piece of raw, sparkling amethyst. This stone shares with me that it represents the part of Mollie's soul that *knows* she is beautiful. The second soul part appears in the form of a vibrant, fragrant sage bush. This is the part of her soul that knows how to walk on the earth in complete harmony with all of Nature. As each soul part is identified, I share what it is, describe its significance, and return it to her by blowing it with strong intention into Mollie's heart space. I sense each breath returning the power and light of Mollie's own soul back to her.

As I work with Mollie—and Alice—soft sobs come from Cleo and Katari. Their tears flow into the peacefulness that envelops the room. The spirits seem to be healing each of us, all at once. I can feel all-that-is, the whole Universe, holding this room and those in it in a sweet embrace, returning us to love and wholeness. Unity.

I softly speak: "Mollie the healing is now complete and you can take your time. Just let me know when you are ready to speak." She remains quiet for a long, long time. I wonder if she's drifted off to sleep. After a while, I gently touch her arm, and she slowly opens her eyes and says to all of us—steadily and clearly, with a smile: "I never knew what baptism felt like until now. Thank you."

A few weeks later, Cleo calls to let me know that Mollie has died. "We burned sage and tobacco in the room as we waited for her body to be taken." I can hear the anguish in his voice. I offer my sympathy and my gratitude for having had the opportunity to know her and to be included in her life. And I thank him for letting me know she has passed.

A few days later, Cleo calls again. He's having a tough time getting words out between his tears. I finally understand that he's requesting that I speak at Mollie's memorial service. I tell him that I am deeply honored and agree to speak. I hang up the phone thinking to myself that I am not exactly sure what he wants.

"It's weird," I tell Mark. "I have the feeling that maybe Cleo wants me to do more than just speak. I think he wants me to do the entire service."

"But why would they want you to do that? They hardly know you," Mark says. I think to myself that he is right. Days later, Cleo calls me again and asks me if, in fact, I will lead the memorial for Mollie. Once again, I agree and tell him I am honored.

Though I know that I'm meant do this, I'm a little afraid, as I've never done anything like this before. I also worry that Anishinabe tribal members may think I'm some sort of New Age fraud, or someone attempting to plunder their traditions. I check in with some of my fellow shamanic-healing friends, one of whom is Native American, and they all put me at ease and remind me that my spirits will help me with all of it. One teases me and says: "The key thing is, because you're a blonde, you need to speak softly to the elders and not make too much eye contact. Oh, and *don't show up drunk*."

I head into my healing room at home, light a candle, and journey via drum to my helping spirits to ask for help. Later, while walking the trail near our house, the spirits give me a prayer from eagle to use as a benediction. I quickly type the words into my phone and email it to myself.

As I plan the memorial service, I think about Mollie's soul and its whereabouts. In the shamanic view of the world, when the soul leaves the body, it can hang around in the Middle World, where there is suffering and pain, or it can transcend and leave this reality for one in which there is unlimited love and compassion, where it can continue to grow and learn. Some souls stick around the earth for a while to deal with unfinished business, appearing in dreams or in other ways to loved ones, business associates, or others. Some stay here by choice, because they believe they can help or care for their ancestors— like the one I suspect I saw in the cave in India. Some are stuck here in this plane because they died accidentally (or in a suicide) and don't yet realize they are dead. These are suffering beings—soul ghosts—who may or may not want help transcending.

I also long for some input from Mollie. How does she want this memorial to look? I suddenly remember that I can ask her. I lie down again, with the drum pulsing in my ear, and ask Alice to take me to her.

Alice immediately takes me to a level in the Upper World, where I find Mollie. She's doing some kind of detailed handicraft in a circle of grandmothers in the deep, cool shade beneath a towering stand of evergreens. These trees are absolutely enormous and the peaceful space beneath them is lush and sweet.

Mollie looks very different from when I last saw her. She looks as if she's in her twenties—vibrant and luminous, with shining eyes—but she has the same warm smile, and I'm able to recognize her. I am overjoyed as I look at her. I know she's already made her transition successfully.

I explain to Mollie that I'll be speaking at her funeral and want her input. She pauses thoughtfully, and then beams: "Tell them how beautiful this place is where I am now and tell them how much I enjoy my work here." Then she smiles and returns to the group of women seated on the deeply shaded forest floor. This exchange puts me at ease. There is nothing sweeter to me than knowing that Mollie's soul is at peace.

I arrive for Mollie's service early and help set things up, placing napkins and punch cups out for the reception. People begin to arrive and fill the rows of chairs arranged in front of a grand fireplace. I stand at the podium and ask that everyone invite whomever they pray to to join us for this hour.

Cleo and both of his daughters, Katari and Donna, speak candidly. Mollie was a really bright light and brought much cheer to her family and to everybody at the Flower Shop where she worked. Donna also shares that Mollie never, ever swore. She had been raised a Catholic and attended strict schools growing up. Apparently, whenever she got really mad or stubbed her toe, she said "fire truck"—anything to avoid an expletive.

Donna tells us about a time when her mother was in hospice care feeling very unwell. She hadn't been herself for weeks. "She had a loud alarm that rang each time she tried to sit up. It was meant to keep her safe, but the alarm kept going off. I kept gently pushing her back down on her bed to remind her to rest. Finally, after a half dozen alarms, my mom said loudly: 'Donna—don't fuck with me.' I couldn't believe my ears. My Dad and I started to laugh—hard. It was the first time I ever heard my mom swear—and the last time I ever heard her speak my name."

The whole gathering laughs with Donna through their tears. Listening to Mollie's daughters speak so honestly about their mom and her love inspires me to go home and be a better mom. She sounds like the kind of mother I am learning to become—softer, more at peace.

We pass a bundle of sage and invite everyone

present to blow their prayers for Mollie and her family into it. After the ceremony, I create a bundle with that sage and Mollie's favorite shirt, something Cleo can keep close to him for the coming year—sing to it and sleep with it. Guided by Alice, I invite him to burn the sage on the one-year anniversary of Mollie's death to mark the end of the formal grieving period.

It surprises me when Cleo introduces me gregariously to several family members and guests by saying: "This is Sarah, our spiritual guide."

PRAYER FOR MOLLIE

May we see the larger view with sharp clarity.

May we see the things our hearts are being called
to and go after them with fierce power and
courage.

May we see our place in the world and how to
live in harmony with all creation.

May we know how to ride the ever-changing
winds and to rest when there is little or no
wind to harness.

May we care for one another patiently and
endlessly—as eagle attends to her chicks.

May we scan the landscape and look for
opportunities to offer our gifts.

May we say thank you—

To the sun that warms us without asking for
anything in return,

To the water for quenching our thirst and
washing us clean,

To the earth and sky for holding us so
beautifully,

To all of the Beasties from mosquito to buffalo
for their contributions to this circle,

To all of the plants for sustaining us,

To the trees who give us shelter and beauty.

And, like eagle, may we know that life is a
circle,

And each of us has a place on the circle.
And when the time comes, may we return with
love and grace.
And so it is.
Miigwech (Ojibway word meaning "Thank you.")

CHAPTER 38

Back to the River

Commit to believing you deserve to
experience all the love and connection
your heart desires. No earning or
repenting or serving time is required.
Elephants never forget this.

Alice the Elephant, in *Born to Freak*

The deluge of rain that arrived earlier today
has moved on. Post-downpour, the June
peonies are standing tall, full to the brim with
tight green buds ready to burst forth. A single
bloom of elephant-tongue pink is just beginning
to show its extravagance.

I walk a few blocks through the neighborhood
and then turn to enter the woods. I stop briefly
to inhale the sweet perfume of a friendly and
familiar clump of Queen Anne's lace.

I invite Alice along, and we head down the
muddy trail together. Alice, with her saggy
pachydermal bottom, leads the way. My own
spirit, ruffled today by endless problems to solve
for the kids, dirty dishes, and a long morning of

editing, is beginning to become more still. I'm soothed by the wet forest and the beautiful clear droplets of rain on leaves and iridescent buttercup blossoms leaning into the late afternoon light. Mark's favorite thimbleberry bushes are already thigh-high and blossoming. I'm aware summer isn't waiting.

Alice and I make it to my favorite rain-swollen river in no time. I realize this river is my Ganges—a place to pray and wash away karma. My thoughts wander back to a recent retreat I led in Thailand, a pachydermal pilgrimage of sorts on which I ended up having another extraordinary teaching from an elephant. This time, it wasn't Alice, but a living, breathing, ten-thousand-pound pachyderm who enlightened me.

We were invited to ride the resident elephants to the river near the inn. They encouraged bareback riding which, we learned, is much more comfy for the elephants than the metal-framed saddles you often see. Knowing the violent history of the domestication of elephants, I was worried about whether riding them at all was a good thing. When I asked Alice, she assured me that *this* ride would be a blessing.

We clambered up onto a rooftop to await our turn to board. When my turn arrived, I noticed that my elephant had large heavy chains around her neck. At first, I didn't want to accept this.

I wanted to be with an elephant who (at least) appeared free. But I realized that it was my turn, and I needed to climb on.

Riding so unsecured atop such a massive beast was terrifying at first. As I relaxed, she kindly tucked her massive ears back over my shins and held me lightly in place. I stretched out my hands and fingers over the bony prominences on her head to steady myself. She automatically began to head slowly toward the rest of our group. As we moved into the forest together toward the river, I could feel my body begin to vibrate all over—a tremor that grew and grew. Then tears started to come. A massive overwhelming wave of love and gratitude was flowing through me. I have ridden on Alice hundreds of times in my journeys, but this was so overwhelmingly and joyfully *real*. My elephant was so gentle and so incredibly full of power, all at once. Her footsteps glided us along through the world; she was so quiet and sure.

Without formal invitation, all of my spirit helpers spontaneously surrounded me; Alice swam alongside us playfully. Their immense lightness enveloped me. They all seemed drawn there simply to witness my joy. "We are so glad you came and trusted!" they whispered in my ear. I have no earthly idea what the beautiful elephant beneath me was thinking; I only hoped she could sense my joy. After a good ten minutes of riding, crying, shaking, and being blissfully blown away by this experience, I noticed my elephant's chains again. This time, however, they spoke directly to me.

These chains told me that they symbolized the heaviness, the burdens each of us carry. Yet, they assured me, each of us is on a journey moving toward more and more freedom. My mind opened gently and new thoughts flowed. We get to choose how we respond to our own perceived suffering. We can choose lightness. We can ask to be unburdened. Like the weighty elephant who swims effortlessly in the river, we too can become buoyant.

Using a few elliptical, curled leaves I find at the river's edge, I make my prayers. For the first, I gather everything that doesn't serve me and send it into the leaf with a single breath. I blow my requests for strength and guidance into the next leaf. With the third, I ask that suffering be relieved for all. The surge of the rain-swollen river carries my prayers downstream.

Alice and I turn and climb back up the bank. As we do, a beautiful slant of late-afternoon light guides us home on the trail, illuminating raindrops on lush green leaves and making the deep blue-purple stocks of lupine glow pink.

CHAPTER 39

Into the Woods—
Then Home

So long as we love, we serve; so long as
we are loved by others, I would almost
say that we are indispensable.

Robert Lewis Stevenson,
Lay Morals and Other Essays

I've been working steadily with different people
who long to be whole again, whose creativity
feels blocked, or who have lost their power and
feel stalled. Some of them are experiencing what
I once did—the feeling that there's something
else, some special work they're supposed to be
doing. It's just that they're not sure what it is
or how to begin. I help them with aid from my
spirits. When they ask, I teach them how to
connect with their own spirits.

So much has changed since I first walked along
the edge of the forest near my house during my
first sabbatical, anxious about the great buzzing
energy I sensed there. I've stopped being timid
and hesitating at the periphery. I now plunge

356

smack dab into the deep woods with awareness.

This fall day, the trails near my house have become brighter overnight with the shedding of dead leaves—as if someone has just switched on the lights. It is the rivers, the stones, the trees, the birds, the flowers, and the sun that are the most powerful reminders to me that we are loved. This beauty—ever-changing, transforming, living and dying and being reborn—is an endless source of inspiration and learning for me. If I've learned anything thus far, it's that my life is extremely blessed and that anything I dream of exists as a possibility. So it's best for me to dream well and be unafraid.

As I walk along, an image of a fetal elephant floating in her watery womb comes back to me. I remember being so touched by the image when I saw it online, because of Alice and all the actual, extraordinary elephants whose families are threatened these days. We may think of elephants as mighty and invincible, but, just like us, they are vulnerable. And right now, all of them need our protection.

On the trail, I stop moving, as I often do when things hit me that feel monumental. Now I see that my musings constitute a great pun from the spirits. Alice, my spiritual guide, is the *elephant in the womb*. She's been there all along. In my mind's eye, I see that spit of land and the confluence where spirit and matter become one, where whatever I consciously want to create or intend can become real with the help of the spirits. I'm held safely and buoyed by these primal forces, just like Alice in her holy sangam.

The pun gains more strength. I can also see that I'm well suited to addressing the elephant in the room (womb) in a lighthearted way, being an upstanding citizen and a doctor, while also admitting to cavorting with elephants in the spirit world, or talking openly about mental illness, or accepting the beauty of death, or confessing to botched breast implants.

My blow-up Dolly Parton shadow has come to represent a perfect photo-negative of my true self—how I give and receive. Her womb represents divine creativity (sexual and otherwise) and her mouth, symbolic of self-expression, represents speaking my truth. I'm here to create and speak my truth.

I feel as if I'm beginning to understand the trajectory of my last few years, yet my journeys still continue to surprise me. One day, I merge with a spirit I know well, but this time it's different. Once again, I am crammed with ecstasy—every single place it can go in my body, it goes. Once again, I am *getting laid by the Universe*. But this time, I'm instructed that the ecstasy and power is to be used for good. It's satisfying to be able to contain this power and not scatter it haphazardly, to be a good steward of it.

This ecstatic experience gets me thinking about my relationship with Mark. Why can't we seem to find more time to be snuggly and intimate these days? I boldly venture a guess over a glass of wine with him: "Do you think it can be that we have both just gotten so spiritual and so satisfied and peaceful in our lives that those cravings have been eliminated? Some Hindu texts talk about the disappearance of sensual cravings being a sign on the path of enlightenment."

Mark laughs and says: "No, I don't think *that's* it."

Suddenly, we're both laughing—together. The desire to connect is definitely here in both of us. It's just that, somehow, we both need to find more ways to let down our guard. But the crazy thing is that just being aware of this doesn't seem to be helping us to acheive it.

I wake up early the next morning with the idea that we could journey together to ask for a healing from our spirits regarding our desire to be able to give and receive love. I stand next to the bed, with our coffee mugs in my in hands.

"Mark," I begin, "what do you think about each of us going on a journey to ask our spirits for healing—for us as a couple?"

"Sounds good to me," he replies sleepily.

"I think our intention should be to ask for a

healing for our relationship and maybe for some advice on what each of us can do to help."

It's nearly 6:00 in the morning, and the house is dead silent except for the birds starting to wake in the backyard. I shut our bedroom door to keep the dog out, and we lie down on the floor, side by side. Mark throws a blanket over himself, and I grab my fuzzy robe to stay warm. I lay my cell phone on the floor between us and start the drumming track.

I travel to the Upper World and make my request. I see Mark and myself lying side by side on the soft ground. My spirits all appear and begin working on us. First, they place a rose in each of our hearts. I have the sense that all of the heaviness between us is being removed. There's a lot of dancing going on around us. And then Charlotte, my spider spirit, begins to weave the two of us together lovingly with the most exquisite gossamer filament, lacing us body to body, spirit to spirit. Over and over, she dives through us and around us, laying down a continuous interconnecting thread. This unusual laced web is invisible yet strong. I'm told that all I need to do is "be myself," which practically makes me laugh out loud. Thank God! I'm tired of trying to be the person I keep thinking Mark wants me to be—more organized, more meticulous, more subdued.

When the drum calls us both back, Mark shares

that, in his experience, he was instructed to "allow"—to be able to receive. Recently, when I tried to hug him or touch him, he sometimes rebuffed me or grew irritated. But he wants to be more receptive now.

I share what I saw. Once again, the space between us has been made tender by the love and compassion of the Universe. We embrace and find ourselves yielding to each other on a new, sweeter, more fearless level. Together, we feel directed to slip beneath the still-warm covers of our bed to love and to be held lovingly by the mysterious forces that join us.

I am home once more.

Acknowledgments

I must begin my thanks with a loving and reverent shout out to God and to the loving and compassionate beings in both the Upper and Lower Worlds. Thank you for all the unlimited love, care, guidance, and encouragement you give me. I hope this work honors you and inspires others to explore the loving realities where you dwell.

I thank Mark for allowing me to write so transparently about his/our private life and for supporting me and loving me. I can't wait to keep getting to know you! I am also deeply indebted to our children—George, Katherine, Josephine, and Charlie—who generously agreed to be part of this book. Each of you teach me to be a better person in your own way. *I love you.*

Mom, I was only able to stay afloat on this project with your help—lovingly reading and rereading the manuscript every time I asked, cleaning it up, and making brilliant comments in the margins. I'm also deeply grateful to you, Dad (the greatest dad in the whole world!), for being willing to do shamanic healing and letting me share your story. I thank my wonderful sister, Maria, for reading rough drafts, for reminding me to show not tell, and for encouraging me to go straight for the enema.

I thank my beloved friend Suzi for calling me on the phone shouting excitedly after reading the first draft. You gave me so much fire and stamina to carry on to the finish. I thank Besty Rapoport for her brilliant editorial shaping and life coaching. Without you, I never would have met Jane Dystel, my wickedly sharp and gorgeous agent, who wisely admonished me: "Less talk and more email, Sarah." Thank you for believing in me—and I am working on it! Thanks to Grace Kerina, who was there at the book's conception and helped me get it to the second trimester. I owe all of my writing to you, as you believed that I could write another book. And thanks to Meghan Fordice, my Mary Poppins, without whose care our family would not be what it is.

I owe a deep debt of gratitude to Cleo Ashworth, Donna Ashworth, and Katari Ashworth-Tafs for inviting me into your lives and trusting me with Mollie's story.

I found many amazing pilgrims along my various journeys, and I thank each of them for taking time to help me understand my experience better: Catharine Larsen, the charming man from Scotland who danced after reading *Born to FREAK*, Yogi Grayhair (Lloyd), Jon (Kosuke) Harada, Jo Anne Harada, Deb Adele, Mary Beth Liesen, Sarah Gorham, Diane Bemel,

Joy Illikanen, M. L. Sather, Kris Thoeni, Joani Nunez, Martha Atkins, Michele Caron, and Nancy Knutson.

I am grateful to Michael Harner for his books, and to the Foundation for Shamanic Studies for their guidance. Deep gratitude to Timothy Cope, my first teacher, and to Alicia Gates, my guide for the three-year program. My life was changed by you. There are no words for the beautiful work you do. A'ho.

Thanks also to the Martha Beck Institute, the tribe, and all of the wonderful opportunities you create. And especially to Martha for daring to write the most helpful and magical books. I am deeply grateful for your encouragement and will treasure my hours at your feet, learning how to write things that can help. To learn more about coach training and other classes, check out *Marthabeck.com*.

This book would not have progressed without the help of many others: Miriam Goderich, Lisa Dunford, Deb Reber, Darla Bruni, Jessica Roeder, Lynn Blaney Hess, Amy Pearson, Lissa Rankin, Mei Mei Fox, and Jaimal Yogis. Thanks to you all.

And last on the pilgrimage, the lovely people at Conari Press/Red Wheel/Weiser Books. Especially to Christine LeBlond for believing in this project and patiently holding my hand as we made the story more lucid and clear. Thanks to the amazing copyeditor Laurie Trufant, whose careful eye was able to see so clearly what I could not, and to Jane Hagaman for taking it all to the finish line. And a special thanks to Kathryn Sky-Peck and your team for the beautiful cover art of Alice and the Taj.

About the Author

The planet does not need more successful
people. The planet desperately needs
more peacemakers, healers, restorers,
storytellers, and lovers of all kinds.

The Dalai Lama

Sarah Bamford Seidelmann is a fourth-generation
physician turned shamanic healer and life coach,
who deeply enjoys shenanigans. She's been a
frequent guest blogger at Maria Shriver's site for
Architects of Change and has led sold-out retreats
combining surfing and shamanism in Hawaii and
a sacred pachydermal pilgrimage to Thailand. She
loves to help others find their own "feel good" so
they can live courageously and enthusiastically.
Visit Sarah at *followyourfeelgood.com*.

Books are
produced in the
United States
using U.S.-based
materials

Books are printed
using a revolutionary
new process called
THINKtech™ that
lowers energy usage
by 70% and increases
overall quality

Books are
durable and
flexible
because of
smythe-sewing

Paper is
sourced using
environmentally
responsible
foresting methods
and the
paper is acid-free

Center Point Large Print
600 Brooks Road / PO Box 1
Thorndike, ME 04986-0001 USA

(207) 568-3717

US & Canada:
1 800 929-9108
www.centerpointlargeprint.com